MARY'S MONSTER

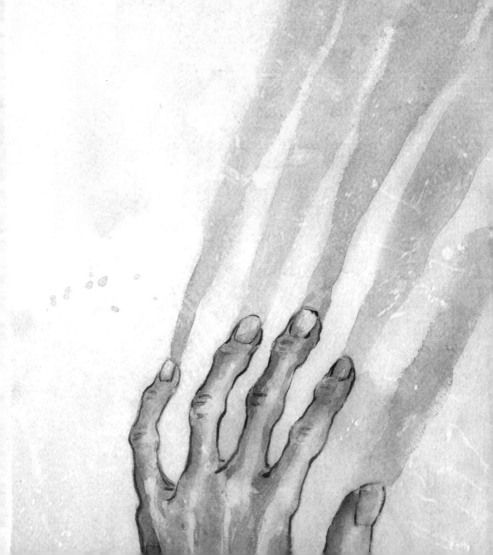

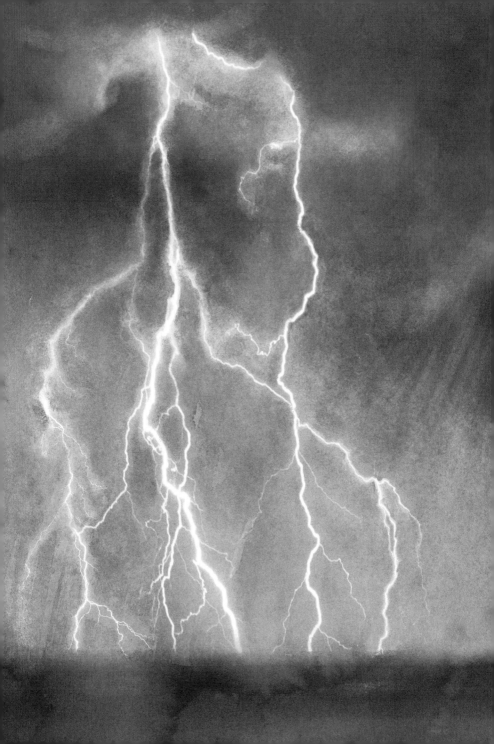

Lita Judge

MARY'S MONSTER

Love, Madness and How Mary Shelley Created Frankenstein

wren
&rook

Copyright © 2018 by Lita Judge
Published in Great Britain in 2018 by Wren & Rook
First published in the US in 2018 by Roaring Brook Press

Excerpt from *Frankenstein* Volume I by Mary Shelley from The
Shelley-Godwin Archive, Bodleian Library, University of Oxford.
Used on p.229, with permission.

ISBN 978 1 5263 6041 0
eBook ISBN 978 1 5263 6097 7
10 9 8 7 6 5 4 3 2 1

Wren & Rook
An imprint of Hachette Children's Group
Part of Hodder & Stoughton
Carmelite House
50 Victoria Embankment
London EC4Y 0DZ
An Hachette UK Company
www.hachette.co.uk
www.hachettechildrens.co.uk

Printed in China

The website addresses (URLs) included in this book were valid at the time
of going to press. However, it is possible that contents or addresses may have
changed since the publication of this book. No responsibility for any such
changes can be accepted by either the author or the publisher.

For Dave,
whose love
and faith
never fail

INTRODUCTION

The novel *Frankenstein; or, The Modern Prometheus*, written by Mary Shelley and published in 1818, is one of the most famous and enduring works of the Romantic era. Nearly everyone has some knowledge of this book, but few know that its author was a pregnant teenage runaway rejected by her family and spurned by society.

In the story, Victor Frankenstein is a science student consumed by an ambition to bring the dead back to life. Using the assembled parts of human and animal cadavers, he succeeds in creating a man but instead of being thrilled, Frankenstein is repulsed by and rejects his creature with no compassion or sense of responsibility. The Creature is left to feel so miserable and alone, he turns monstrous. Mary's novel is a cautionary tale, warning readers of the horrible outcomes that can result when man attempts to conquer nature. It is also a radical social criticism.

Defying the restrictions of her day, Mary was brimming with ideas that women were equal to men and that all people were entitled to justice and freedom. She ran away with a married man, Percy Bysshe Shelley, who was a poet with radical political beliefs. Together the young couple fought against social conventions by daring to believe love and human reason could reform a tyrannical world. Mary also changed the course of literature. She invented the Industrial Age science fiction novel, sculpted the first mad-scientist archetype, and delivered the most iconic monster ever to have been created.

Mary's Creature has inspired writers, filmmakers and theatre producers for the past two hundred years. Say 'Frankenstein' and most people will conjure a vision of the monster. He has been altered in later adaptations, devolving from an articulate and intelligent soul to a groaning, lobotomised version of himself. Even the way he is referred to has morphed from namelessness to a being with the surname of his fictional creator, Frankenstein. But the themes in Mary's story remain, and it is a testament to her creative genius that she developed a creature so indelible, he lives on eternally.

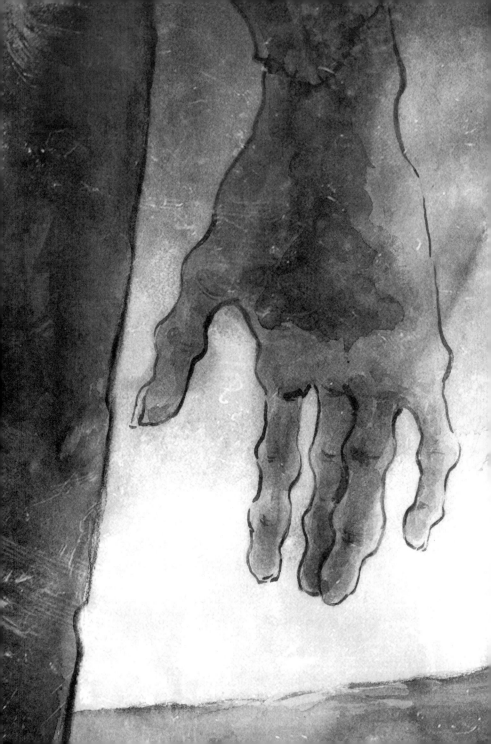

PROLOGUE

THE CREATURE

Most people didn't believe Mary Shelley,
a teenage girl, unleashed me,
a creature powerful and murderous
enough to haunt their dreams.

They expected girls to be nice
and obey the rules.
They expected girls to be silent
and swallow punishment and pain.

She was cast out from society
because she loved a married man.
Her friends reviled her.
Her father banished her from his home.

But she did not hide.
She was not silenced.
She fought against the cruelty of human nature
by writing.

4

She conceived me.
I took shape like an infant,
not in her body, but in her heart,
growing from her imagination
till I was bold enough to climb out of the page
and into your mind.

Now Mary is the ghost
whose bones have turned to dust
and it is I who live on.

But hear her voice!
She wrote my story,
and now she will reach beyond the grave
and tell you her own.

PART I

EXILE

JUNE 1812

A great proportion of the misery that wanders, in hideous forms, around the world, is allowed to rise from the negligence of parents.

- Mary Wollstonecraft, *A Vindication of the Rights of Woman*

Do Not Return

Early summer, in a time of war,
when the sea is a battleground
and ships are weapons,
I find myself on the deck of the *Osnaburgh*
heading for Scotland.
Little separates me from the mail
and cargo in the ship's hold.
I am like a letter stamped DO NOT RETURN,
being delivered to a future I cannot know.

I try to keep the shoreline in sight, as if this
will prevent the wind driving the sails.
But gradually, the land recedes into a thin line
and then is swallowed completely
by bruise-coloured clouds.

I am left to feel
completely alone.

MEMORIES

The memory of my father's face haunts me.
His mood was as dark as the sea when he put me on board.
My stepmother hadn't even come to see me off,
nor had my brothers, who were away at school.
Only my sisters, Fanny and Claire, cried a little
as the ship pulled away.

At the thought of them I reach for the purse
that hangs at my waist.
It holds their letters and the coins Father gave me.
But my chilled fingers come away empty
and my despair sinks deeper.
The purse is gone.
It is an unpleasant reminder that I,
a fourteen-year-old girl travelling alone,
am easy prey for pickpockets and thieves.

I grip the rail tighter,
holding myself up on trembling legs.

How have things come this far?

THE FAMILY I LEAVE BEHIND

No one was kinder to me than Fanny.
She was only three years older than me,
but had been forced to be both mother and sister
since the day I was born,
because our mother had died.

From the earliest I can remember it was she alone
who wrapped soft, warm arms around me
and held me when I cried.

HERSCHEL'S COMET

Father used to tell me how he watched a comet with a tail of flame
hurl itself across the London sky
on the night that I was born.

That comet was like a messenger heralding a new era,
its path illuminating a line between old superstitions
and mankind's growing understanding of the planets and stars.

But the almost impossible fact about that comet
was that it was discovered
by a woman.

Caroline Herschel was an astronomer,
self-trained,
because women were barred from universities.

She toiled and laboured
until she had named eight comets
and no one could deny she was a scientist.

Father gave me the belief that I could do anything
when he told me the story of the comet
that blazed across the London sky

on the night that I was born.

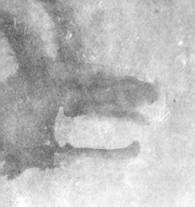

A Childhood of Poems

Father didn't expect us to sew,
or play with dolls like other girls.
Instead he gave us the books our mother had written
and encouraged us to read.
He taught us independence is admirable,
and imagination indispensable.

Fanny and I were allowed to stay up late
when Father's friends came over to discuss science,
and politics and literature.

My favourite friend was Mr Coleridge,
who could make even Father laugh
with his game of making shadow creatures
dance on walls.

Then Mr Coleridge would put down his hands
and his thoughts turned inward and dark,
and his liquid voice recited poetry
spooky enough to summon witches down our chimney.
But all of this ended when Father remarried.

Without a Word

One morning eleven years ago, Father left
to collect that loud and awful neighbour who called herself
   the Widow Clairmont,
even though she had never married.
Without a word to us, he took her to church and made
   her his wife.

That afternoon she marched into our home looking
   plump and pleased,
like a dog who has stolen another dog's bone.
Her daughter, Claire, and son, Charles, followed behind,
looking as confused and sullen as Fanny and me.

The New Mrs Godwin

Father's wife shouted at our laundry girl,
and bickered with the butcher.
She gossiped about the neighbours
even though she had her own secrets to hide.
She had been an unwed mother and spent time in
   debtors' prison.

Father didn't notice her temper at first.
He only saw Mrs Godwin smile when he passed her in the hall
and gave her gentle pats on her round bottom.

It wasn't long before she grew even fatter
and delivered Father a son whom he named William Jr.
All his talk of girls being able to do everything boys can do
seemed to vanish.

Debts

Father had money enough
to give to any friend in need,
mostly other writers
who had fallen on hard times.

Father was their champion,
publishing their work
even if it didn't sell
and giving them something to live on.

But as soon as our family swelled
from three to seven mouths to feed,
debts began to stack up
faster than the books Father wrote.

No Longer My Home

I sneaked downstairs like a stowaway
and crept beneath the couch
to listen to Mr Coleridge
recite his poem
The Rime of the Ancient Mariner.

I imagined I was riding a ship
across an icebound sea

when Mrs Godwin spied me
and dragged me out by my hair
and hissed that I was an awful child
in front of Father
and all of his friends.

HOLBORN

1805

It was Mrs Godwin's idea
that we leave our home in Somers Town,
where the scent of meadow jasmine
slipped through our windows.

It was her idea that we move
into an abandoned shop in Holborn,
where Father's lost dreams haunted the halls
alongside ghosts of thieves and murderers
who hung from the gallows at Newgate Prison
a block from our door.

It was her idea that Father could get out of debt
by writing and publishing children's books
that we would sell in the little shop
below the rooms where we lived.

Father Wasn't Meant to Keep Shop

He was the first to call himself an anarchist.
Observing the plight of the poor and oppressed,
he challenged the world to overthrow tyrannical monarchies.
He wrote books on political justice and believed people could evolve
above cruelty through love and kindness
and rule themselves without governments or kings.

During the time of the French Revolution,
politicians in England turned to Father for his ideas.
But a reign of terror followed in the years after rebellion,
when corrupt revolutionaries became despotic,
unleashing public beheadings and merciless violence.

The bloodshed stained the reputation of anarchists
and people grew afraid of reform.
Father was labelled a notorious radical.

GREEN-EYED DEVIL

Mrs Godwin didn't scold Claire
for preening her raven-black curls
instead of helping me unpack endless crates of books.

She said Fanny and I would do without singing lessons,
but demanded that Father pay for Claire's
because her daughter was as gifted as a lark.

Mrs Godwin didn't say a word of praise
when I recited long poems, but shouted at me
about how I combed my hair and which dress I wore.

There was nothing I could do
except be silent and stare
when her anger poured over me.

My silence only made her madder.
Like a green-eyed devil with her green-tinted glasses,
she slapped me hard across the face

and then stormed into Father's study
to interrupt his work
and report every detail of her little life.

Exile

She convinced him that I must be sent away
to learn to control my temper, even though she is the one
who does all the screaming.

Now Father is cold and remote toward me
because he is too worried about mounting debts
to learn the truth of her jealousy and meanness.

And I am alone on a ship
carrying me
farther and farther
from home.

PENANCE

During the days I am cursed by sea and sickness,
but this isn't as difficult to bear as the nights,
when I am forced below deck
to the tiny cabin
that feels like
a prison.

BECAUSE I DO

I lie shivering in my berth.
My ragged breath is as if a monster
breathes within my ribs.

In ... out ... in ... out ...

I grip my legs and arms
to make myself small.
But I can never be small enough
to stop thinking ...
These are the limbs that ripped through my mother.

In ... out ... in ... out ...

For ten days after my birth
my mother battled to live.

In ... out ... in . . . out ...

But she no longer breathes,
because I do.

SIX DAYS AND NIGHTS

Memories of my childhood follow me
as the ship carries me to Scotland
to live with a family,
a widower called Baxter
and his daughters.

I have never met them,
but they once wrote my father a letter
saying they liked his books
and wanted to be of service to him.

Father replied by suggesting
they take me in.

36

PART II

MY SECOND BIRTH

JUNE 1812-MARCH 1814

My dreams were all my own; I accounted for them to nobody; they were my refuge when annoyed - my dearest pleasure when free.

- Mary Shelley, 1831 Introduction to *Frankenstein*

A New Home

I expect to find Scotland grey and dreary,
but instead frothy white waves race toward land and crash on shore
as if they are in a hurry to leap above the cliffs
and explore wild green hills climbing high enough to touch the sky.

Mr Baxter and his four daughters greet me kindly
and take me to their home at Broughty Ferry,
where I am thankful to find the stone walls of their cottage
warmed by kindness and laughter.

The girls talk eagerly of how they admire my mother's writing.
They ask a thousand questions about life in London, and the sea
    voyage,
and what my father is like, for they've never met him,
even though they've read every word he has ever published.

At last I can no longer hide how tired I am.
They jump up and spin around me,
unpacking my bag and putting extra quilts on my bed
in the room I will share with Isabella, which
    they've already made pretty
with sweet-smelling flowers.

ISABELLA

Isabella and I spend long, perfect afternoons
exploring the twisted alleys of nearby Dundee.
She shows me the alehouses where Highland rebels meet in secret,
planning their attacks on the English troops who rule their soil.

We walk to the high mound on Guthrie Street
where a century ago, girls accused of witchcraft
were burned by the scores.

She leads me to the harbour,
where ships return from the Arctic
heavy with the stench of whale oil
and stories of shipwreck and mutiny.

Her greatest passion is the French Revolution.
Isabella has read so many biographies of its leaders,
she talks of them as if they were friends.
On dark wintry days when we are driven indoors,
she stages operatic performances of brave and tragic heroines
who were forced to the guillotine, like Madame Roland.

Standing above her sisters, she makes a grand speech
and swoons when she gets to Roland's final words,
'O Liberty! What crimes are committed in thy name!'

Then Isabella falls on her sisters
and they sob and giggle together,
and I would have been homesick for Fanny

if they didn't turn to me then
and tell me again
the story of my own mother's life.

41

MOTHER

Mary Wollstonecraft was mother to a rebellion
before she was mother to me.
As a young woman she left her home in England
and braved mobs and bloody riots to run headlong to France
to witness the birth of liberty in the midst of revolution.

Growing up in a time when there were no laws
to prevent her father from beating his wife,
she rose up from a childhood of abuse,
and dared to be the first to denounce unfair laws toward women
with her book *A Vindication of the Rights of Woman.*

She continued to devote her life to future generations of women
by writing novels with fearless heroines.

My mother challenged a world of angry men
with the soft feather of her pen.
Bayonets and cannons weren't her weapons of war.
She chose words alone to begin her revolt.

Her words were formed by courage.
Her stories were her victories.

THE BOOKS MY MOTHER WROTE

I search through the Baxters' library for the books
that my mother wrote. My mind grows within the cradle
of words preserved in her novel *Maria*.

> *Death may snatch me from you, before you can weigh my advice, ...*
> *I would then, with fond anxiety, lead you very early in life*
> *to form your grand principle of action ...*
>   *Gain experience – ah! gain it –*
> *while experience is worth having, and acquire sufficient fortitude*
> *to pursue your own happiness; it includes your utility, by a direct path.*

Her thoughts and ideas reach across the space of time
and come alive and lodge inside my chest
like my own heartbeat.

As if I have been given a second birth,
her dreams become mine.

ALMOST TWO YEARS

My stay with the Baxters
was planned to last six months,

but six months turns into a year

and a year turns nearly into another.

I am sixteen.

During this time Father writes
precisely once a month
to admonish me to strengthen my character
and reinforce again that I not be an inconvenience.

Occasionally he suggests I return home to help in the shop,
but I no longer encourage him.

I have found a home here
upon the misty moors and woodless mountains.

I have found a sense of belonging
next to the warm hearth
of a new family.

POETRY AND NOVELS

My hands continue to pore through books
giving me glimpses of different worlds.

My heart chases freedom alongside fighting clansmen
in Walter Scott's *The Lady of the Lake.*

My feet plunge bare into cold crystal waters
   of Highland streams
while I read Wordsworth's account of
   his Scottish travels.

My mind descends into hell
with Milton in *Paradise Lost*

and climbs up to the stars
in reading about Herschel's discoveries.

I read poetry and novels
and scientific journals.

I read everything I can find
because they all promise
adventure
sacrifice
love
freedom

life
as my mother had wished
for me.

SCOTLAND HAS BECOME MY EYRIE OF FREEDOM

The wind is my friend,
the sea my sister,
the mist drinks my tears,
and stars hold my hopes.

A thousand gales rage
before Father insists
I come home again.

I am no longer a girl
weary with disappointment.
I have become rock
and wind and fiery sea.

49

PART III

RETURN TO DARKNESS

MARCH-APRIL 1814

31 March 1814. The allied armies, with the Emperors of Russia and Austria, together with the king of Prussia at their head, enter Paris, dethrone Bonaparte, liberate the Pope, proclaim the restoration of the Bourbons, in unison with the French people, avow civil and religious freedom, and announce peace and harmony to the whole world.

- John Evans, *A Sketch of the Denominations of the Christian World*

AN END TO WAR

All of London is celebrating the day I come home.
This is no spring-day kind of jubilation.
This is a reckless insanity,
the kind that follows the wreckage of war,
when everyone goes crazy from the sheer relief
that the world hasn't come to an end.

But I cannot join in their relief.
My heart is too heavy missing Isabella
and I worry over what I will find at home.

Chains

Father looks sunken as he leads me home.
Only he sees that this victory over France
is no end to suffering.

Once, Father dared to hope
that the French general Napoleon Bonaparte
would bring reform to corrupt monarchies
after France had fought a revolution
and beheaded its corrupt king at the guillotine.
But instead of reform, Napoleon crowned himself emperor
and amassed an army to march across Europe.

England had to ally itself with Russia and Prussia to stop
this mad emperor from taking over the continent.
Nearly two decades of war followed,
leaving much of Europe in ruin.

Now, like a serpent shedding her skin,
France rips off the shackles of its insatiable emperor
and exchanges them for the chains of another king,
brother to the king it beheaded before,
All of Father's dreams for reform are dead
and another senseless war has 'come to nothing.

BACK TO SKINNER STREET

I walk in the black wake of Father's mood,
trying to hold on to memories of the wind
  and sky
above the green Scottish hills
as the stench and squalor of Holborn
slam into me like a fist.

The din of carts over cobblestones
will never be loud enough to block
the sound of cattle screaming
as they are led to slaughter.
Here, at Skinner Street, where we live,
even the end of war can't stop
gutters from buzzing with flies
and running with blood.

Instead of coming home,
I feel
as if I've been shipwrecked.

DREAMS OF REMEMBRANCE

I stand at the entrance of our door,
where the room seems dark
and the bookshelves bend,
more with the weight of disappointment
than with books.

CLAIRE

My stepsister is fifteen now and has grown
into a young lady while I was away.
I am startled when she springs toward me
and throws her arms around me, as if my coming home
is the most wonderful thing to ever happen in her life.

We fought bitterly when we were young,
competing for little scraps of attention from our parents.
But her tight embrace makes me think her life has been hard
these past two years, and suddenly I want to forget all
that came between us before
and start anew.

FANNY

Fanny looks the same,
a little thinner perhaps,
and paler,
her head bent forward,
her eyes cast down.
She greets me kindly,
but I can't help feeling
like we have become strangers
in the way she steps
nervously toward me
and quickly pulls away.

GRATEFUL

I sink into Claire's embrace,
comforted by the tight grip of her fingers
curling around my arms,
and the feel of her warmth
pressing against my chilly skin.

I am exhausted
and sick to my stomach from six days at sea,
but her friendly chatter lifts me up the stairs
and guides me into bed.

I drift into sleep feeling grateful
that we can be sisters again.

63

A Spiritual Son

In the days following my return
my family talks of little but a young poet
named Percy Bysshe Shelley.

'He is the son of a wealthy baronet,' Claire tells me
and he vows that his essay *The Necessity of Atheism*
has been inspired by Father's philosophies.

For two years, Shelley has been writing to Father.
Now he promises to visit.
Everyone rereads his letters to me
as if they hold a sacred hope.
Shelley's plan to lend Father money
could be our family's salvation.

'He calls himself a Godwinian,' Claire says.
'Even more, he promises to love Father
as would a spiritual son.'

The Screaming

Each day Mrs Godwin's shrill voice cuts
through the thin plaster walls of my father's study.
I see nothing has changed. She still berates him endlessly
over the mounting debt and failing business.

This morning she is tearing up his letters from friends
because, she says, they are a distraction,
and waves menacing threats from creditors,
as if he doesn't already feel the looming dread of debtors' prison.

I go back upstairs so she won't aim her cutting words
and stinging slaps in my direction,
but mostly because I am sickened to see my father,
a man once so commanding and influential,
shrink beneath this unworthy woman.

A BURDEN

When Fanny was eleven and I was eight,
Father gave us the memoir he wrote about Mother
and we learned that
we were only half sisters.

Fanny had a different father,
who was already married
and abandoned our mother
to go back to his wife.

'Father only wrote about Mother's secrets,' I told Fanny,
'because he was proud
of her choice to love freely.'

But the secret that broke Fanny's heart
was that Mother tried to drown herself twice
after Fanny was born.

Now I see that Fanny felt alone while I was away.
The hurled insults from Mrs Godwin
without me to fight back
have fostered another terrible secret.

Fanny believes she is a burden
to parents
who don't see her as their own.

I No Longer Belong

I am home less than a month
and the sense of belonging I felt in Scotland
has become memory and tears.

I miss the sound of the reckless sea.
I miss feeling like a bird who rides the salty air,
gliding on a wind of possibility.

I miss the brightness of Isabella's smile, and most of all
I miss my mother,
because she felt alive to me there.

And I wonder if I will ever
find a family
that will feel completely my own.

PART IV

The Poet

May–July 1814

Soul meets soul on lovers' lips.

- Percy Bysshe Shelley, *Prometheus Unbound*

SHELLEY

The day Percy Bysshe Shelley
walks into my life
is as if a bolt of lightning
shoots through my soul.

My heart
had been like the Holborn sky,
thick and cold
and the colour of coal.

Then in an instant,
a crack of thunder
and the entire landscape
of my existence changes.

A HUNGER TO GIVE

He visits Father almost every day.
I see longing in his eyes
and a sadness that tinges his voice,
revealing an endless hunger
to put his position and wealth to good use.

Perhaps, I wonder, he feels too much
the burden of his privileged birth.
He is only twenty-one years old, and already he has given away
most of what belongs to him.

Now his wife, Harriet, has left him,
and still he promises to borrow more
against his future inheritance
to give to Father.

A SECRET

I wait each afternoon for him to walk through our door.
His clothes smell of mist and leaves and musty sweat
and his soft brown hair twists
as though he had been dancing with wind,
and a little of the careless breeze
follows him inside our shop.

I want to reach out and tuck one restless curl
behind his ear and let my hand linger there,
at the back of his neck,
and I blush when I see his lips curl
slightly, as if he can read my mind,
because I know at that moment
a secret has passed between us.

His Gift

One afternoon as I work
behind the bookshop counter,
he hands me the book he wrote, *Queen Mab*.

When I am alone I open the cover
to find the long poem was inscribed to Harriet,
but he has crossed out her name
and written mine in its place.

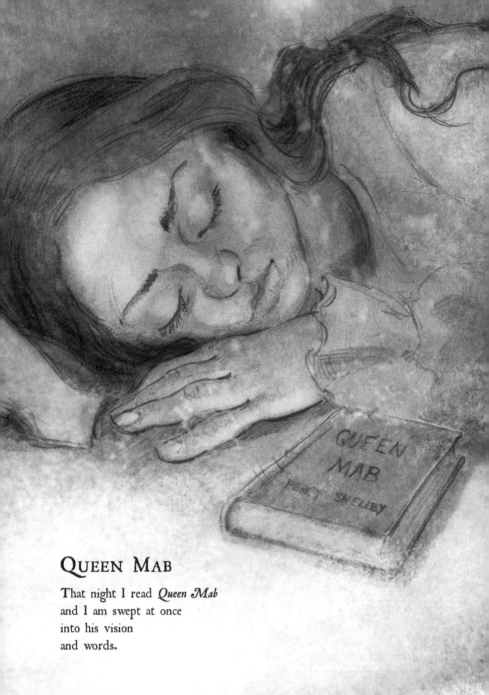

QUEEN MAB

That night I read *Queen Mab*
and I am swept at once
into his vision
and words.

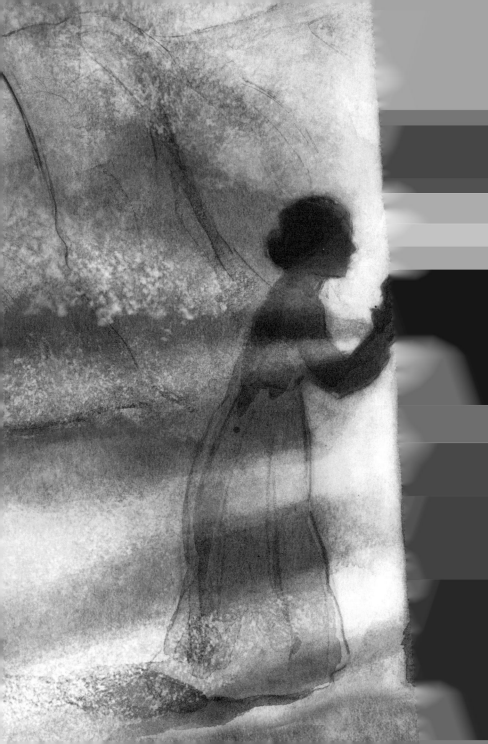

His cantos
sound like trumpets
to a prophecy

that a better world
will begin
naturally,

through love
and imagination
rather than wars.

WITH FATHER'S PERMISSION

JUNE 1814

One Friday evening after the shop is closed,
Shelley accompanies Claire and me for a walk
down to the river at the edge of Holborn,
where the breeze is crisp and smells of life
instead of prisons and slaughterhouses.

Suddenly my mind is doing somersaults
as I race to keep up with his quick steps.
I lean in closer as he describes peering
into solar microscopes at living matter.
I tell him I have read of Herschel's discoveries of comets and stars,
and then ideas are spinning around us.

Shelley leaps to point out that he performs chemical experiments.
Even as a boy, he studied galvanism, or electrical current,
and I laugh when he tells me he accidentally set the butler on fire.
Shelley believes scientists will someday use galvanism
to bring the dead back to life.
I believe we are only beginning to understand all the things
science will teach us.

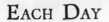

Each Day

I count off hours
working behind the counter,
waiting for when Shelley will course through the door
pretending to have another important matter to discuss with Father,
then prolonging his visit
so we can walk together again.

Claire joins us, but drifts behind,
as galvanism,
alchemy,
gravity,
astronomy
become a secret language
to Shelley and me.

I Don't Want to Fight

Fanny stares at me
after I say Shelley has told me his marriage is over.

'They have a child together,' she says.
'Harriet waits in her father's home to deliver him a second one.'

I remind her, 'Father teaches love,
not marriage contracts, should bind people together.'

Fanny raises her voice. 'She eloped with him when she was sixteen!
Don't trust Shelley when he says she doesn't love him.'

I don't want to fight. So I pretend to agree,
while inside I'm wishing she'd remember
she'd never have been born if Mother
hadn't had the courage
to love a married man.

My Mother's Grave

27 June 1814

Shelley and I walk alone
under a rose-coloured sky
to the sacred place
where my mother lies buried.

He carries my mother's book *Maria*,
but he doesn't open it.
Instead, Shelley recites passages
that he knows by heart.
And then I know we share so much more
than a love of science and poetry.

MOONRISE

Under a sky deepening to night Shelley pours out his anguish
that Harriet never loved him,
that she cares only about his money
and inheriting the title of baroness,

and that his family rejects him and wants him committed to an asylum.
He tells me his father would prefer he join the army
and die in the ditch of some foreign war
than see wings grow from his poet's soul.

And all at once I see how desperately Shelley needs love.
It isn't hunger to relieve others' suffering that tears him apart.
It's his own anguish gnawing a gaping hole
through his heart.

WANT

I want to hold Shelley
with the force of an eagle
taming the wind within its wings.

I want to grasp him unfailingly,
like a gentle moth
dancing with flame.

I want to have strength enough
to beat off the beasts
that dwell within his heart.

I want to believe
in impossible promises
and shift the world
so they can be kept.

I want to be more
than a girl
selling books
in a bankrupt shop.

MARY WOLLSTONECRAFT
GODWIN
AUTHOR OF

BESIDE HER GRAVE

My heart is beating louder than black-eyed birds
cawing a violent desire for life not death
as I tell Shelley we can do the impossible,
we can love each other and make our own rules.

And when I feel the warmth of his lips on mine,
  I know
that like my mother and father,
who fought a revolution of ideas,
Shelley and I will fight our own
and set the world on its edge.

OUR LOVE IS REAL

I lead him under the long limbs
of the willow beside my mother's grave.
We lie down together

within this hidden world seen only by ghosts.
Then Shelley is on top of me
and inside of me, and everything hurts,

except the pain that has burned within me
my entire life.
That deep ache is lifted,

because now we are a part of each other,
and no matter how we will be judged
for our actions,

we will run away together
and love each other
and that is the only thing that matters.

BETRAYED

I thought Father would defend my decision
to live with Shelley.

But Father says nothing when Mrs Godwin slaps me
so hard across the face my skin feels burned
and my bones bruised.

'He's in love with the idea of your mother,' she shrieks,
'more than with you!'

Their rage is complete with hysterics
and slamming of doors, but in truth,
they are beggars
sending me to my room
while they invite Shelley back
to ask for his money.

BROKEN PROMISES

Father promised
freedom, love, equality
for women.

But for me, it seems,
he has locked the door
to any future
beyond selling books.

Choosing Between Loves

Fanny doesn't talk to me about Shelley anymore;
instead, her silence shouts disappointment.

I know she feels wounded, she's a little in love with Shelley herself,
but it isn't jealousy that fuels her glare.

No, she's worried that if I run away our family's reputation
will be tarnished even more than it already is.

I'm hurt she believes Father is right.

I'm hurt she is forcing me to choose between loving her
and loving Shelley.

A HOME OF OUR OWN

Each night I shiver with desire to be in Shelley's arms again.
He promises we will leave England
to live in Switzerland.

Rousseau and Voltaire, free-thinkers both, lived there.
Along with other expatriates,
Shelley says we will escape
the rigid constraints of England.

But most of all he picks Switzerland
because Father chose it for his hero,
who left his loveless marriage to run away with
    a sixteen-year-old girl,
in his novel *Fleetwood*.

I am sixteen, just like that girl!
Even if Father now shrinks from his ideals,
Shelley and I will follow in the path
of his characters.

I Won't Leave Her Behind

Claire passes secret letters between Shelley and me.
Together we stay up late whispering,
planning my future.

'Take me with you,' Claire pleads
when I tell her we are leaving soon.
'I can't live in this tomb any longer!'

Claire is like the swifts who sleep restlessly
within the chimneys. Little birds
who huddle together in the blackness of night,
clinging to soot-covered stones,

but at dawn they rise
on thin, sturdy wings
and carry the sun
up into the sky.

I tell her that I will never
leave her alone
to live in this house
where there is too little love.

Helpless

Father forbids me to leave my room
and intercepts the letters I send through Claire.
I am helpless to stop the anguish
that must be growing in Shelley's heart.

He waits outside the shop for Father to leave,
then bursts through the door,
runs upstairs gripping a bottle of opium,
and sinks to his knees, sobbing,
'Swallow it all!'
He holds a pistol to his head.
'Then I will shoot myself
so we will never be parted.'

I hold his trembling body
and I vow I will not break my promise
to run away with him.
But he must leave now,
before Father comes home.

Under a Midnight Moon

I write Father a letter
and place it on his desk,

and then, like two ghosts
slipping from a graveyard,
Claire and I run to Shelley,
waiting in a rented carriage.

Through night and day we race,
as if the devil himself chases us,
and reach Dover late the next evening.

FLIGHT

Black clouds gather ominously,
but Shelley fears our being followed
more than being drowned.
He hires a fishing boat to take us immediately
across the sea to France.

The wind builds, cursing our flight,
tossing angry waves to swamp the boat.
All night, Claire and I cling to Shelley,
terrified we will sink to an icy grave.
But Shelley challenges the wind.

At last the storm exhausts itself.
A bright, warm sun welcomes us to Calais
as Shelley carries Claire and me to shore.

PART V

Six Weeks of Freedom

Summer 1814

I felt the blood that burn'd
Within her frame, mingle with mine, and fall
Around my heart like fire.

- Percy Bysshe Shelley, *The Revolt of Islam*

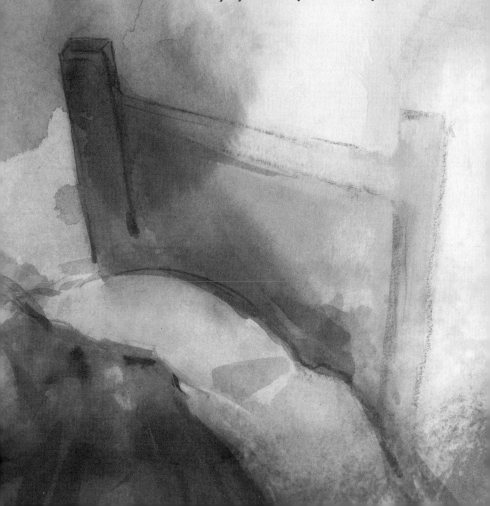

IN PARIS

Shelley and I lie for hours in each other's arms,
making love, reading poetry
and writing in the journal
we have begun together.

Our dingy room has broken windows and dirty sheets
because Shelley was in such a hurry to leave
he forgot to bring much money.

I don't mind.
Claire has her own room,
and Shelley and I are alone
at last.

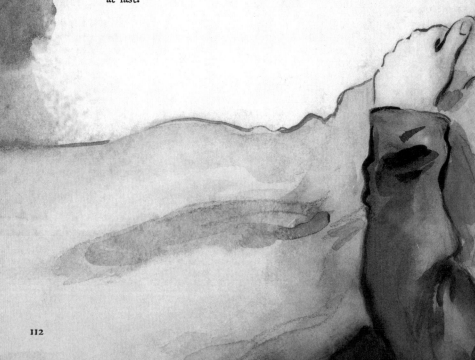

THE SOULS OF STARS

During the day we live as flower seeds floating on sunshine,
drifting through streets that twist like labyrinths,
gazing at stone buildings the colour of gold.

At night we write poems,
then fold them into paper boats and light them on fire,
as if to equip them with the souls of stars.

LEAVING FOR SWITZERLAND

Shelley's father has blocked all banks
from lending him money,
but Shelley reassures me,
'We don't need money.
We are poets,
anarchists,
prophets;
our pockets need only be filled
with love for the universe.
We will drink sour milk and eat stale bread.
We will walk over mountains!'

SON OF EARTH

The little donkey Shelley bought to carry our trunks
sinks to his knees and we must drag him pitilessly
until we can trade him for a mule.

My feet grow blistered, my muscles burn under black silks
and blazing sun as we walk nearly thirty miles each day.
Shelley marches on

as if hunger and heat and exhaustion
can't touch him,
until he sprains his ankle.

Then Claire and I
have to carry the trunks filled with books
while Shelley rides our mule.

'Life,' Shelley calls out,
'is like living in
a Wordsworth poem!

'I am a voyager,
wandering lonely as a cloud,
forever meant to live a solitary existence.'

Claire and I, feeling the weight
of the trunks, are too tired
to respond as Shelley shouts,

'I am Son of Earth, Orphan to Storm,
flung out by society to wander over the world
in search of the sublime!'

I Find No Sublime

When I was a girl I loved looking through books
of France with pictures showing beautiful pastures
and milkmaids tending cows. I remember drawings of brave peasants
with pitchforks raised, fighting invincibly for liberty.

Now I walk through the French countryside
and see only a nation ravaged by two decades at war.
Here the villages are burned and the fields are barren.
The only crops that grow are gravestones and ghosts.

Even Shelley's thoughts grow quiet
and forbidding as we walk
over endless miles
of suffering.

The children haunt me most of all.
Their bones are bent,
their bodies deformed.
I am ashamed to be repulsed

by their rancid rags and lice-ridden hair.
It is man's unquenchable thirst for power
and violence that is truly ugly,
not these miserable children.

Images of the poor
pile up like waves in my imagination
and threaten to drown me.

We Find No Inns

Maybe it is the heat, or fatigue from walking
all the way across France in the past three weeks,
or the despair that drifts deeper into my mood,

but I grow light-headed and sick to my stomach,
unable to sleep in an itchy hayloft
or on some poor farmer's hard kitchen floor.

No matter how thin I have become, I can't force myself to eat
the meagre breakfast we find of stale bread
soaked in water, barely soft enough to chew.

Into a Grey World

At last Shelley agrees to rent a carriage
to take us over the steep slopes of the Alps.
We rise among snowcapped peaks,
envisioning a little chalet where we will live
beside water as blue as heaven.

But before we can glimpse Lake Lucerne,
smut-coloured clouds muscle themselves
in front of the sun and release
curtains of rain.

The only cottage we can afford
is rat infested,
damp, with a broken stove
that refuses to light.

I shiver in wet clothes,
my thoughts turning as grey as the world.
How long will this go on
before we can go home?

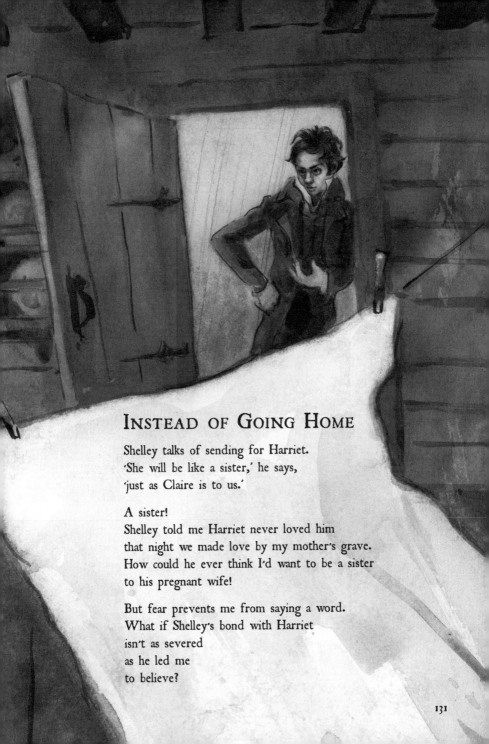

INSTEAD OF GOING HOME

Shelley talks of sending for Harriet.
'She will be like a sister,' he says,
'just as Claire is to us.'

A sister!
Shelley told me Harriet never loved him
that night we made love by my mother's grave.
How could he ever think I'd want to be a sister
to his pregnant wife!

But fear prevents me from saying a word.
What if Shelley's bond with Harriet
isn't as severed
as he led me
to believe?

DREAMING OF FANNY

At night my dreams are restless.
I see Fanny alone, in the room we shared.
I see her sitting with me by a river,
smiling at a baby I hold in my arms.
Then I am flying above Fanny's still body,
as if she were dead
and I scream awake!

I shiver in an icy sweat, trembling, I think,
because my heart is aching for her,
until another wave of nausea grips me
and I clutch my stomach. Then I realise,
I am not just exhausted and feeling dreadful
for leaving Fanny.

I am pregnant with Shelley's baby.

133

MAYBE

Maybe Father will forgive me
if he knows I am expecting a child.

Maybe he will realise my love for Shelley
is no different than his love was for my mother.

I hold on to this hope as I reach across the bed
to wake Shelley and tell him we will soon have a baby.

But instead of holding me and telling me how happy he is,
Shelley puts on his boots and stomps out the door.

I am left alone, praying that his dark mood
is only because he worries we are nearly out of money.

Turning Back

Not until hunger and cold
seep into our bones,

not until Claire screams because of the rats
that crawl over our beds,

not until I grow weak with the baby growing inside
and argue miserably with Shelley

does he agree
it is time to go home.

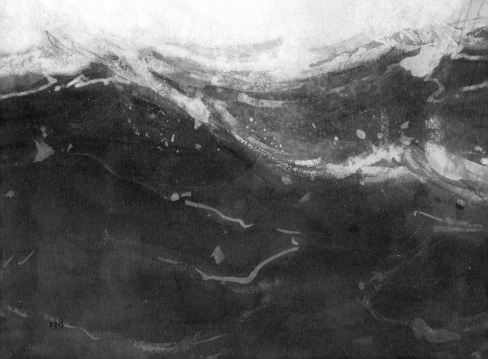

PART VI

RETURN TO ENGLAND

SEPTEMBER 1814-MAY 1816

My heart was fashioned to be susceptible of love and sympathy; and when wrenched by misery to vice and hatred, it did not endure the violence of the change without torture such as you cannot even imagine.

- Mary Shelley, *Frankenstein; or, The Modern Prometheus*

A SPECIAL CURSE

Banished,
outcast,
rejected
forever.

There is a special curse
reserved for girls
who dare to run away
without a wedding ring.

People I have known
my entire life
turn their backs
and slam their doors.

But that sorrow doesn't wound
like the pain when Father
forbids me
to enter his home.

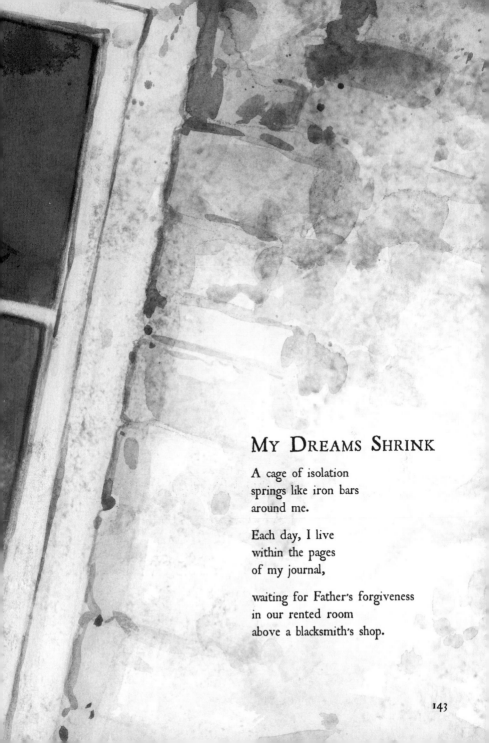

My Dreams Shrink

A cage of isolation
springs like iron bars
around me.

Each day, I live
within the pages
of my journal,

waiting for Father's forgiveness
in our rented room
above a blacksmith's shop.

I Am Alone

Winter 1815

It wasn't enough for Father to pretend not to know me
when he passed me on the street.
Now he's written to Isabella
and turned her against me.

Even sweet-natured Claire grows irritable with me
when I say we must save what little money we have
to buy bread instead of coal.
'You exile us to a cold prison,' she snaps.

But what does she know of true exile?
She won't be branded for bearing a child out of wedlock.
I can no longer walk the streets because of my thickening waist,
while she can still go into town with her brother, Charles,
home now from school.

Only Fanny breaks my loneliness by writing to me.
But I sink deeper into despair with her melancholy letters.
It is Mrs Godwin who keeps Father's anger fuelled.
Fanny will be cast out if she dares to visit.

SINKING UNDER DOUBTS

I can't tell Shelley how unhappy I am
because his own thoughts
snap at his heels like hounds.

He says he must stay away during the day
to hide from bailiffs who hunt him for unpaid bills.

At night he comes home
gripped by his troubled emotions.

I grow worried that his feelings of persecution
go beyond keeping ahead of debt collectors.

147

A Knock at the Door

Shelley hears footsteps in the hall
and leaps out the window
to escape the terror that stalks him.

He wanders endlessly,
challenging faceless devils to appear in dark alleys.

When he returns, he sits alone,
raking in his fear like the embers of a fire,
feeding his thoughts until they catch flame
to fuel his poems.

PAIN

Shelley believes words can heal
the pain of an entire world,
but I begin to fear
they will never heal his own.

This realisation makes the ground
 beneath my feet
feel as if it were slowly giving way,
 like grains of sand
being swept adrift by waves inexhaustibly
beating themselves against the shore.

I can't stop the creeping sense
that no matter how much I love Shelley,
someday we will all be drowned
in his pain.

LITTLE PIECES OF ME BEGIN TO HATE

Because Harriet spreads gossip that my father
has bartered two daughters
for fifteen hundred pounds.

Because I can't stop thinking how my birth
   caused my mother's death,
and I begin to fear what fate awaits me
upon the birth of my child.

Because Shelley has begun
to look at Claire
the way he once looked at me.

My heart withers
and my tongue sculpts bitter words
that only make me feel ugly and unloved.

WOULD HARRIET PITY ME?

Does she know how much I fear Shelley will leave me
each time he walks out our door
to visit her and the newborn son she has delivered?

Would she forgive me if she knew my father
never will?

Would her hatred for me lessen
if she felt the knife of sorrow cut through me
each time I think of her and those we have hurt?

PARTED

Fanny walks across Holborn,
her fingers blue in the numbing cold,
her skirts heavy with mud.

When she comes to our door,
she stands silent, shivering,
her eyes filled with tears.

My heart pounds with hope
as I reach out to hold her,
but then she turns and walks away,

disappearing
into the pewter-coloured sky
like a ship adrift in an icy sea.

CLARA

22 FEBRUARY 1815

Seven months after Shelley and I ran away,
our daughter, Clara, is born.

Two perfect eyes look up at me in shock,
as if to ask - *Is this life?*

Suddenly, I understand. I didn't steal my mother's life
when I was born.

She gave it, just as I have now given
my daughter life.

Ten Days

For ten days she drinks milk from my breast
and I feel her warmth against my skin.

For ten days I cradle her in hope and joy
and caress those little fists that grip my hand.

For ten days she lives,
just as my mother lived when I was born.

But she was born too soon. Her lungs
weren't ready for life outside my womb.

I clutch her, helpless, when the convulsions come
to steal the life from her tiny limbs.

Tears

Tears do not come at first.
Only a silent sob
that builds into a howl.

Like a wounded animal,
I scream and scream,
until exhaustion
numbs my aching throat.

Then the dreams come.
I hold Clara's body by the fire
until the flames revive her.

Her soft blue eyes open.
My baby is brought back to life
in my tormented sleep.
When I wake, I must live
the nightmare of her death
all over again.

I Am Seventeen

Already
I am daughter to a ghost
and mother to bones.

SPRING

Instead of remaining by my side,
Shelley and Claire walk out together
under blankets of apple blossoms,

leaving me alone and tortured
by thoughts of sweet flowers
growing from my baby's grave.

I feel so hurt that Shelley doesn't grieve
for our daughter.
Even more, I feel injured

that his love is like a breeze blowing through trees,
setting leaves to dance
before ripping them from their limbs.

IT ISN'T A GAME

At night I go to bed alone while Claire stays up late
playing her favourite game, being Shelley's new mistress,
singing to him, giggling,
and begging him to tell her stories.

But stories aren't a game to Shelley.
After midnight, when he sips his opium
and watches the hot tongue of fire die down to coals,
glowing embers fill his eyes
and darkness fills his heart.

Then the hunted becomes the hunter.
Like a sorcerer casting a spell,
Shelley weaves stories of witchcraft and ghosts
so sinister Claire convulses with fear.

Suddenly she is pounding on my door,
sobbing and begging to come in and sleep in my bed
after she has already
been in his.

I Pity Her, I Hate Her

I drag my aching limbs from bed
and wrap them around her.
My words are as soft as silk,
but inside, I feel like nettles and thorns.

My heart fills with hate
that Claire is Shelley's new lover,
that we have become rivals,
no longer sisters.

And suddenly rage
instead of emptiness
threatens
to swallow me.

Emotions Left to Me

Anger

when Father writes to Shelley to say he won't condone our life,
but demands more money from us
because he hears Shelley has received his inheritance at last.

Despair

over Fanny, knowing she feels hopeless to escape,
because the stain of scandal when two sisters live
   with a married man
tarnishes the reputation of the sister left behind.

Bitterness

because Claire and I now hate each other so much,
screaming isn't enough and we resort to smouldering silence.

Life feels like a tomb.

I sink deeper into thoughts of how easy it would be
to follow my baby, Clara, to the grave.

But when I ran away with Shelley I knew
life with him would require faith in our belief that love
can be given freely.

I want to believe in the purity of this idea,
though it brings so much pain and suffering.

I am not just an unwed girl.
I can choose to forgive.
I can choose to live again,
broken but breathing,

half lover, half pain.

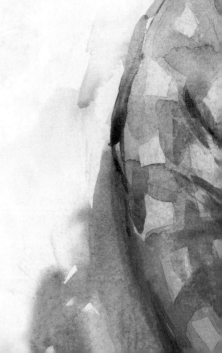

LOVING SHELLEY

In the following months
Shelley and I
find our way back
to each other.

I devote myself
to giving him
the kind of love
he needs.

Claire is his sister again.
Only I can soothe
Shelley's nerves.
Only I can share
in his poetry.
Only I can give him back
his dreams.

BISHOPSGATE

AUGUST 1815

We have come into an inheritance
from Shelley's grandfather
and can leave the rancid stink of Holborn
to rent a house in Bishopsgate,
where there are trees, and meadows,
and the songs of birds,
and where this time,
when I tell Shelley I am expecting another child,
he agrees to send Claire away
to stay with his old housekeeper.

For the first time in our lives,
Shelley and I learn what a real home is.
Home is not an address
with fine curtains
and fancy furnishings.
Home is a place in the mind where thoughts
grow rich enough to become stories,
breaking the silence that exists between souls.

HOPE ENOUGH

In the morning I write in my journal.

In the afternoon Shelley and I ramble,
drifting quietly through the ruins of an abbey,

or we lie down together
under the shade of an ancient oak.

Then, like a nightingale with a sweet song,
Shelley reads the long poem
he has written, entitled *Alastor*.

I believe again,
hearts that hear his notes
will be moved and softened

and we will find hope enough
to live the life
we imagined.

I Am Eighteen

January 1816

Less than half the age my mother was
when she gave birth to me,
I deliver my son, William.

From the bloodied sheets of childbirth,
his gentle spirit enters our lives
and brings more love to Shelley and me.

Motherhood

I balance a book in one arm,
reading aloud to Shelley
while holding William in the other.

I whisper away demons
and sing soft lullabies.

I stay up late into the night,
working to the low flicker of an oil lamp,
copying Shelley's scribbled poems on to clean paper.

I rise each morning to wash nappies and mend clothes
while my mind weaves my own stories
I have no time to write.

CREEPING FEAR

When *Alastor* is published
we have such high hopes
that Shelley's work will be recognised.

But reviewers ignore his poetry
and write only scathing criticisms
of his 'subversive behaviour.'

I grow worried
darkness
will overtake him again.

CLAIRE IS BACK

FEBRUARY 1816

Claire comes home unexpectedly.
She lifts William, swings him in her arms,
then melts to the floor, tickling him and giggling,
while telling me her plans to sing professionally
or make a career in the theatre.

I don't say much, but I think to myself,
Becoming an actress is a good idea.
After all, Claire loves being dramatic.

She keeps interrupting my thoughts,
asking how I've been,
telling me she's missed me.
I don't want to believe a single word,

but her eyes fill with tears,
and her hands shake,
and she begs me to forgive her
and suddenly I hear myself saying she can stay
a little while.

I know I'll never love her like before,
but she tries so hard to make amends
and I pity her isolation.

Each day, we take small steps
toward, once again, being sisters.

Mad, Bad and Dangerous to Know

Claire insists I come with her to meet her new friend, Lord Byron,
who has connections with the theatre.
'Don't worry,' she says,
'he's even more scandalous than we.'

Of course I already know this.
Lord Byron's *The Corsair*, his poem set in a Turkish harem,
was an epic success, selling ten thousand copies
the very morning it was released.
But the man is more famous than his work.

Newspapers make him sound like the devil incarnate.
Readers pretend to be horrified by his recent divorce
    while rushing to buy
more papers filled with stories of his debauchery and scandalous affairs.
Now he is reported to be living with his half sister, Augusta,
and even to have fathered her child!

Secretly, I resent that people still invite him into society
even though everyone calls him mad, bad and dangerous to know.
It's because he's a man,
and a man, it seems, can behave very badly,
while a woman must hide herself away if she breaks the rules.

Still, my heart goes out to Byron.
Since I was a girl, I've read his poetry
and I know how hard it is to live life as large as a poem.
Shelley admires him like a god.

I can't resist going with Claire to meet him
after she tells me Byron is a huge admirer of my mother's writing,
and has read *Queen Mab*
and thought it very promising.

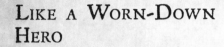

LIKE A WORN-DOWN HERO

I come home and tell Shelley
Byron is no debauched devil,
as the newspapers depict him.

He is just like us, believing poets
must push their powers of invention
to dream up lives
beyond the hypocrisy of conventions.

Shelley grows excited as I tell him
Byron is leaving England.
He will spend the summer in Geneva,

and he has invited us to join him.
Shelley and I and Claire
decide at once
to retrace our path to Switzerland!

188

PART VII

❦

WILD HEARTS

No man chooses evil, because it is evil; he only mistakes it for happiness.

- Mary Wollstonecraft, *A Vindication of the Rights of Men*

GENEVA

We cross over mountains again,
believing we can climb the shoulders of giants
to touch the sky.

When we descend out of a world of ice and snow
into the valley of Lake Geneva,
mist rises to reveal mountain peaks
sheltering us like friends,
and silent lightning flashes
like thin-limbed dancers.

Switzerland is a different world
than the one we saw before.

WAITING

We check in at the Hotel d'Angleterre and drift
into a lazy routine, reading by a crackling fire
and playing with little William in our rooms
while we wait for Byron.

In the evenings we walk downstairs,
past marble statues so lifelike
they look as if they could leap off their pedestals
and spin around us and dance arm in arm.

We enter the dining room, where porcelain,
silver and crystal cut glass sparkle
like jewels under candlelit chandeliers.
Then we eat poached apples, sweet as nectar,
floating in cream, and thinly sliced potatoes
dripping with cheese, and bread as light as air
until we are so full we can barely eat another bite,
except to manage a few more spoonfuls
of iced sorbet.

SAILING

One afternoon the weather clears
and we race across the lawn and
fling ourselves into a boat.

Shelley shouts out poems as Claire and I giggle
because the wind whips our bonnets off
and makes our skirts flap so much
we feel like we'll soon fly.

The day wanes and the wind calms
as if it has grown tired of playing with us,
and leaves us to ourselves, floating
placidly.

I lean over the side of the boat
and watch slim minnows swim beneath the emerald water.
That evening, drowsy and happy, we drift back to shore
under a bright-faced moon climbing the violet sky.

Claire takes William to bed
leaving Shelley and me to walk alone,
drinking in the thick scents of butter-yellow flowers
and honey-sweet grass.

On a Stormy Night

25 May 1816

Well past midnight, two weeks after our arrival,
all of the guests are awoken
when six horses thunder down the Alpine road,
pulling Lord Byron's Napoleonic carriage.

Byron, mud splattered and foul tempered, sweeps in
like an emperor, shouting orders to servants
who jump to unload a string of carriages
that have pulled in behind.

Suddenly the lobby is a torrent of commotion.
Eight enormous wolfhounds,
five cats, three monkeys,
an eagle, a crow and a falcon
are unloaded and brought inside.

Byron's carriages also bring enough china and silver
to host his own dinner parties, an entire library,
trunkloads of clothes, art, wine, even a stash of soldiers' bones
he has collected from battlefields,
and his personal physician, Dr Polidori.

SOLDIERS FOR ART

Byron comes sailing with us.
At first his mood is as sullen
as the lead-coloured sky,
but I watch brightness enter his eyes
when Shelley talks about imagination
and his belief that poetry
can be used as a weapon
against tyranny.
'We must write,' Shelley shouts,
'to lift literature from the shackles
of convention!'

'Critics are idiots,' Byron shouts back,
'to ignore your work!'
And suddenly it is as if they are soldiers
charging a blood-soaked battlefield,
willing to fall on their swords
and die for their art.

Sails snapping,
waves crashing,
I rejoice
to see Shelley
looking strong,
looking
happy.

CLAIRE FLIRTS WITH BYRON

In truth, I like her flirting with him.
I don't discourage her even when it's apparent
he's bored by her advances.

I am grateful for her new obsession.
I think it will keep Shelley closer to me
if she amuses herself with the dream
that she might claim her own poet.

I tell myself Claire's heart won't be broken,
it's clear to all Byron isn't searching for love.
For him, passion is simply an experience
like the brandy he drinks
and the opium he smokes
to numb hidden sorrows.

What harm, I ask myself, will come
if she enjoys an innocent crush?

LIKE FALLEN ANGELS

We grow weary of hotel guests
whispering tiresome rumours.
Can't they just leave us alone?

Their gossip that Shelley keeps two wives
has grown dog-eared.
Now they create more fanciful tales
that he's found an English lord
to join in our bed.

We refuse to remain another day
providing entertainment
for their insipid lives!

Byron has rented the Villa Diodati
from the family that hosted John Milton.
And there is a little cottage right next door
where Shelley and I can stay.

We depart at once
to live like fallen angels
in Milton's *Paradise Lost*!

VILLA DIODATI

The weather grows worse,
driving us indoors.

At first it is fun.
Shutters banging,
rain pouring,
wind howling,
candles blowing out.
We gather by the fire
to read Dante's *Inferno*.
We debate the meaning of Greek mythology,
and Prometheus's eternal punishment.

Then Byron's mood grows even more macabre
and he turns to reading ghost stories
from a book he found in the villa.
But he grows disgusted by the weak plots
and throws the book down.
'I challenge you all
to write one of your own!'

LIKE A VAMPIRE

Dr Polidori lingers on the fringe of our circle,
a happy servant ready to contribute
to our discussions one minute,
then sulking the next.

Byron enjoys the young doctor's company
when Polidori enlivens a rainy evening
recounting ghoulish tales from medical school,
detailing students lurking in cemeteries,
robbing graves. Byron leans in to hear more
about stolen cadavers and forbidden dissections.

But then he grows bored
when Polidori reads from a play
he has written about vampires.
'What a fool,' he sneers.

STORMS BUILD

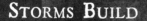

JUNE 1816

The newspapers relate that a foot of snow fell in Italy,
and crops have frozen from China to America.
Reporters predict millions will starve this winter.
People begin to fear that the sun itself is dying.

Shelley and Byron debate scientific reasons for the thunderous weather.
They believe a volcanic eruption a continent away
spewed enough ash to block out the sun.

Their discussion builds over how long clouds of ash
can circle a planet.
I don't join in their debate. I think only of the suffering
we saw on our first journey through France.
Then, it was an army that sowed famine and death.
Now, it's a volcano.

Life and mountain-making
are endless battles
between the forces of destruction
and the forces of creation.

SHUT INDOORS

A week of pounding rain shuts us indoors.
I grow afraid our darkening paradise
is sinking Shelley into another black mood.

His temper flashes swift as lightning.
'The rich could end famine if they cared anything
about the plight of the poor!'
His voice cracks like claps of thunder.

Byron snarls, 'Your bourgeois notions
are no longer amusing.'

Shelley grows more agitated.
'Rich men cast food to their dogs
while young children starve!'

Byron isn't even paying attention.
He is like a hound grown bored with his bone,
turning to tease Polidori again.

I try to calm Shelley's nerves,
but no matter what I do or say, it isn't enough
to stop him from slipping into his private hell.

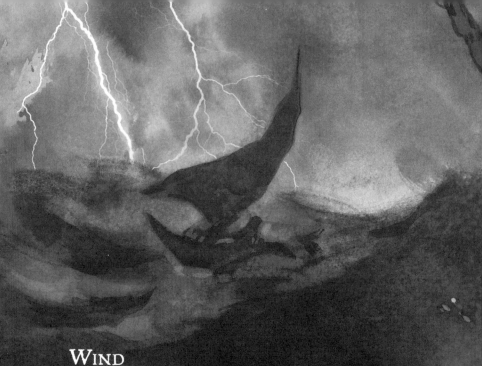

WIND

The lake has turned
into a boiling cauldron
and angry waves call out to Shelley,
compelling him to sail again.

He screams into the wind.
As if he has a raven's wings,
he gathers it in his arms.
But the wind is deaf
to his poet's cry.

Life for Shelley has become an odyssey of emotion,
a sea of love and anger and fear and loneliness
that swamps his mind.

I fear someday the wings of his poet's soul will fall away
and the weight of dread that grips him
will lead him to a watery grave.

CAROUSEL OF NIGHTMARES

16 JUNE 1816

The lightning is too sinister for us to walk back and forth
to our own cottage so we spend the night at the villa,
where the men stay up talking about death,
and cadavers and galvanism.

Like a nervous rat, Polidori jabs at Shelley's thoughts.
'I have seen scientists,' he says,
'animate the corpses of dead dogs with electricity.'

Shelley's eyes glisten in their bruise-coloured sockets.
His mind holds a thousand thoughts of what is real
and what is beyond imagining.

He shouts, 'Man, perhaps, not God,
could bring the dead back to life!'
He slams his fists so hard against the table,
the plates rattle like bones.
'Galvanism will allow men to create life!'

215

WHAT DO MEN KNOW
OF CREATING LIFE?

I am sickened they talk so easily of men,
not women,
creating life.

It is men, not women, who march with armies
across countries, pillaging and burning villages,
leaving children to starve.

Now, men aim their ambitions on conquering nature?
Shelley and Polidori are wrong to envision such things.

Science gives us the ability to pull back the skin of life
and reveal the truth of things. It allows us to understand
the mysteries of mountain-making and falling stars.

But knowledge isn't meant to be held as a weapon
in a battle to defy our fates and manipulate
    life over death.

Evil lodges too easily in men's hearts.
What will happen if they assume the power
to create life?

I CAN'T STOP THINKING

Shelley's words
echo over and over in my thoughts.

Man, perhaps, not God,
could bring the dead back to life.

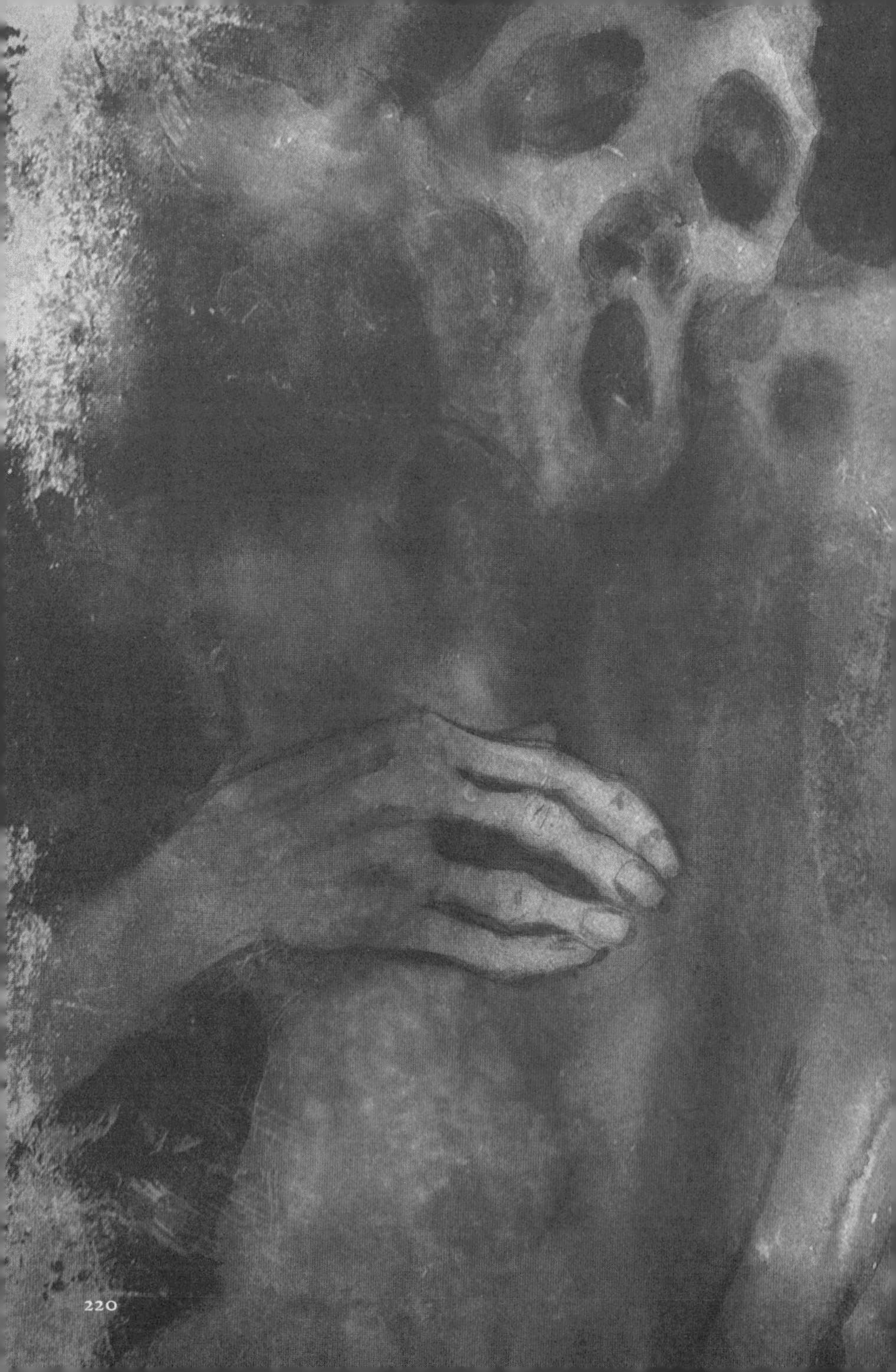

Dead dogs.
Animated corpses.

The dead back to life ...

HEART POUNDING AGAINST RIBS

Cold sweat drips down my spine
as I am seized by a wakeful dream.
I see a pale student of unhallowed arts
kneeling beside the thing
he has put together.
A hideous phantasm of a man
with watery eyes and blackened lips
stirs with motion.

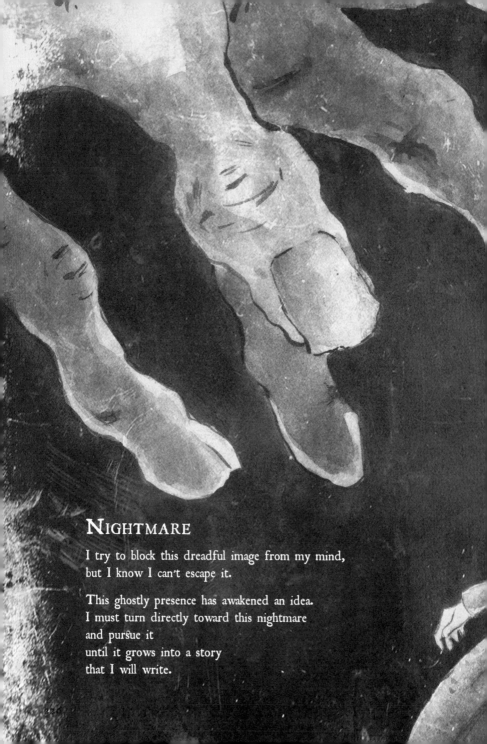

NIGHTMARE

I try to block this dreadful image from my mind,
but I know I can't escape it.

This ghostly presence has awakened an idea.
I must turn directly toward this nightmare
and pursue it
until it grows into a story
that I will write.

SHADOWS TOUCHING

At first, writing feels like falling
where there is nothing to hold on to
to keep from slipping off the edge of the world.

But then the dark presence of another begins to whisper
from the corners of my mind,
and his shadow grows and touches my own.

Together, we take one step toward finding a word,
and then another,
and another,

until the struggle drops away
and the only thing that is left
is everything that matters.

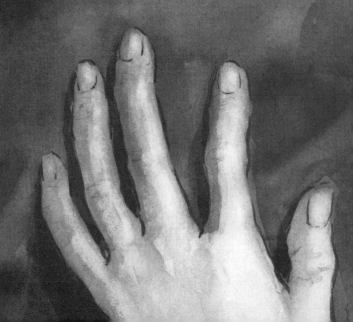

Chapter 7th

It was on a dreary night of November
that I beheld the ~~frame on who~~ my man compleated. And
with an anxiety that almost amount-
ed to agony I collected ~~the~~ instruments of life
around me ~~and endeavoured~~ that might endeavoured to infuse a
spark of being into the lifeless thing
that lay at my feet. It was already
one in the morning, the rain pattered
dismally against the window panes &
my candle was nearly burnt out, when
by the glimmer of the half extinguish-
ed light I saw the dull yellow eye of
the creature open — It breathed hard,
and a convulsive motion agitated
its limbs.

~~But how~~ How can I describe my
emotion at this catastrophe, or how deli-
neate the wretch whom with such
infinite pains and care I had endeavoured
~~to~~. His limbs were in proportion
I selected his features ~~beautiful~~
~~me~~, great God! His
& the work of

CREATING A WORLD

I show Shelley the words
that have spilled across my pages
and he grows excited.

Our love revives
within a creative storm
that unites us.

He believes in me!

Even Byron says my story
has great potential.
Our tensions ease.

We are once again allies,
fighting for literature
instead of against each other.

LIKE A METEOR

On a perfect evening when the sky is mild,
Shelley suggests we celebrate my nineteenth birthday
a few days early by waltzing with flames.

We fly into motion sewing muslin
into a hot-air balloon. Then we run
to the top of the hill and launch it on fire.

Like a meteor
it rises against the blackened sky
to the Milky Way.

233

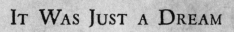

It Was Just a Dream
26 August 1816

Claire is in love with Byron.
Now she is expecting his child
and he rejects her.

I am furious with him,
and with Shelley,
who has known for a month.
They've already discussed Claire's fate
behind her back.

After the baby is born,
Byron will take it.
Claire can do nothing to prevent this,
because the injustices against women
that my mother wrote about
are still in place.

BYRON'S MOOD IS LEADEN

He binges on brandy
and grows unkinder by the day,
tormenting Claire with stories
of dead mistresses
and discarded lovers.

But I think he is truly monstrous
when he threatens to cast her baby aside
by sending it to a convent
if it is born a girl.

CAST OUT TO HELL

29 AUGUST 1816

I know the greatest pain a mother can face
is losing her child,
but I can't prevent Claire's pain.

All I can do is plead with Shelley
to return to England
so we can get her away from Byron.

PART VIII

Deeper into Nightmare

SEPTEMBER 1816-MARCH 1817

Her voice did quiver as we parted,
      Yet knew I not that heart was broken

From which it came, and I departed.
      Heeding not the word then spoken,
            Misery - O Misery,
                  This world is all too wide for thee.

      - Percy Bysshe Shelley, *On Fanny Godwin*

HIDING

We move to Bath, a city far enough from London
to keep Claire's secret from her mother.
A bleak autumn unfolds
as she and I wait for her baby to be born.

I can do nothing to lighten Claire's spirits.
All she does is cry and write letters to Byron,
hopelessly pleading with him to kindle love.

My own spirits are dampened
because Shelley stays in London most of the time,
fighting with bankers about overdue loans
and arguing with Harriet about money.

But I won't live within caged walls anymore.
I march over Alpine glaciers.
I ride icy waves on faraway oceans.
I live within the pages of my growing novel

until I receive a letter from Fanny.

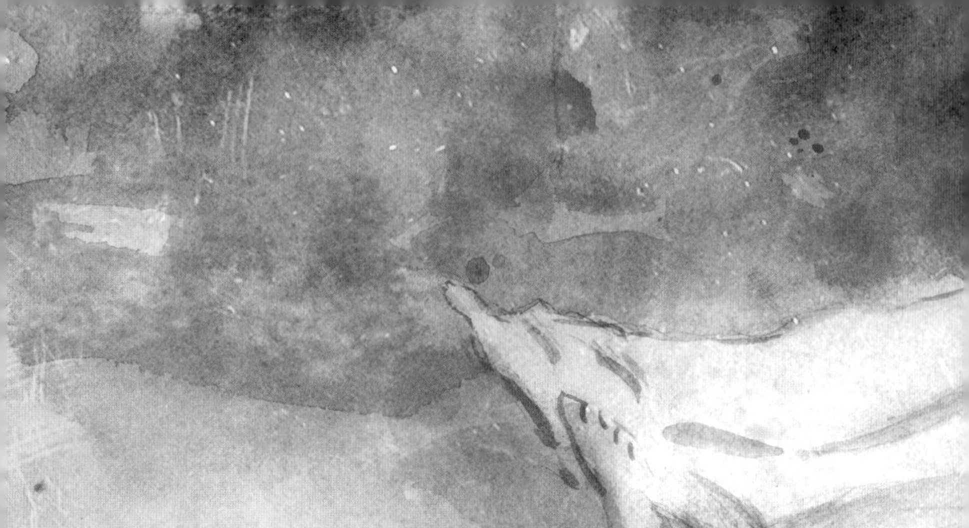

WHY, FANNY, WHY?

9 OCTOBER 1816

Did Mrs Godwin make you feel
too much a burden
as Father sank deeper into debt?

Did you believe you'd never find love
after I destroyed our family's reputation?

Fanny, did you die looking to the stars,
praying Shelley and I
would rescue you?

We received your letter.
We raced to find you.

But it was too late.

You had already swallowed
the bottle of opium.

You chose death
far from home,
alone,
in some rented room.

FATHER'S LETTER

Father wrote a book about my mother
and told the world she tried twice to take her life.

He made sacrifices to tell his truths.
Sacrifices, he taught me,
are the cost of courage.

Now Fanny is dead, and Father lies!
He tells everyone that Fanny is visiting faraway friends
and writes to forbid me to claim her body.

Later he plans to lie again,
and say she died of fever.

Father lies.
And his lies condemn me
to silence.

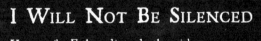

I Will Not Be Silenced

How easily Father discards the girl
he raised as his own child!

He forces me to abandon Fanny
to an unmarked grave,

but I will not abandon her memory!

The grief,
and guilt,
and anger,
and truth
I feel about her death
weave into the characters of my book.

I keep writing as death
continues to circle around me.

HARRIET

10 December 1816

Next it is a boatman's hook
that dredges Harriet's rotted corpse
from the river Thames.

SUICIDE

When Shelley tells me her death
is branded a suicide,
I want to fall into his arms
and at the same horrible moment
beat my fists against his chest.

I can do neither
because he leaves immediately
to learn the details.

I don't want details.

I already know too much.
My breath catches in my throat
each time I try to gulp air
past the swallowed horror
that I caused her death.

Just as if I had hunted her down
and pushed her helpless body into the river,
I am to blame.

Lies He Tells Himself

I receive a hysterical letter from Shelley
telling me she was pregnant.
He claims she was insane,
and that she sank into a life of prostitution
after her father drove her from home.

I know these are lies he tells himself.
Like the lie that Harriet never loved him.
Or that he didn't wound me deeply
when he slept with Claire after our baby died.

Rumours are already spreading
that the child was Shelley's.
Harriet's father never abandoned her.
He gave her a home
when Shelley deserted her.

Blaming Harriet's family for her suicide
is just another lie he tells to shield himself
from the pain lodged within him.

DEATH FILLS
MY DREAMS

My sleep is tortured
with horrific images.

Fanny's corpse forgotten,
without a gravestone
to mark the existence of her life.

Harriet's hair flowing in black water,
eyes swollen, staring
straight at me.

My daughter's tiny fists
turning blue
and releasing their grip.

I feel as if my own soul
is buried in their graves.

Grief would swallow me
if it weren't for the story
still growing in my mind.

DO YOU HEAR ME?

I keep writing
until my pen scratches pain
as loud as screams.
But it is no longer my own voice I hear.
It is the Creature's.
Ink-black words on paper
  are no longer words.
They breathe and pulse with a life
  of their own.
They are heart and legs and arms
and hands made of flesh and bone,
and they reach down my throat
and into my lungs,
and grab my breath
and squeeze out my tears,
until they become the Creature's own.

His voice calls out to me,

Now, Mary,
  You begin to see.

I Am

I am an exiled girl who feels so rejected by her father
she must create a family from ghosts.

I am a poet who feels persecuted
because society loathes him for his beliefs.

I am a sister shackled by illegitimacy and despair,
lying down to die alone.

I am an abandoned wife standing beside a river,
no longer able to endure living.

I AM the rage and shame
that burn like embers through you.

I AM THE WORDS torn from your mind
until they pulse like a BEATING HEART.

I am your Creature

My Creature is me!

Learning How to Breathe Again

Creating is bone crushing,
like the limbs of an infant
pushing through a mother's body.

It is heart beating,
like a newborn baby
held in your arms.

It is miserable
and beautiful,
like learning how to breathe again.

I Write

Till my fingers take up the ache
my heart can no longer hold,

till my broken hopes and crushing sorrow
inch toward bearable,

till the words save my soul
by creating your own.

FEARLESS

I call up phantoms
from voiceless graves
and make you my Creature.
You make me wretched.
I make you strong.
You make me vengeful.
I make you loving.

You Create Life

You shape my horrific screams
from the slaughterhouse cries you heard as a girl

and fashion my gruesome frame
from the corpses of convicts you saw strung up in Holborn.

Inside your mothering form,
an infant is beginning to grow,

while you build me from a dead man's limbs
and sculpt me from a criminal's bones.

Your child grows safe and warm,
listening to her mother's pulse,

while you make my chest beat
with a dead man's heart.

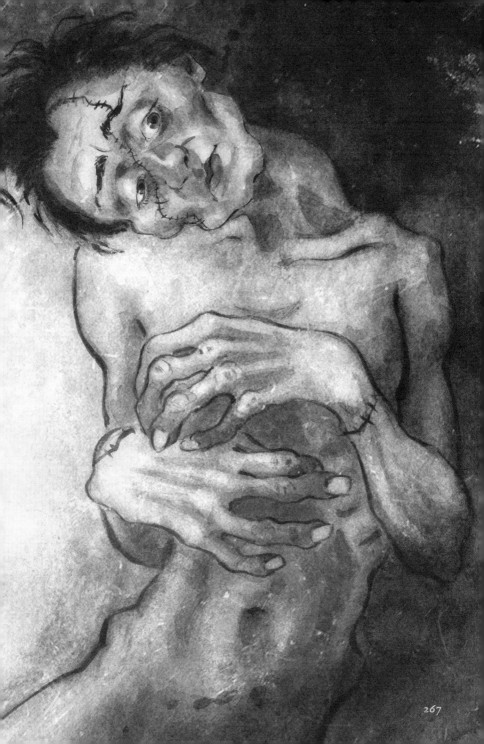

THESE CHILDREN

Yes, my womb holds an infant again.
But this child and Claire's, recently born,
are no different from you.

They will be scorned and considered loathsome,
because people reject those who don't fit
their vision of a perfect ideal.

Already my son, William, is branded a bastard,
as if his innocent life
is less treasured than others.

As long as evil grips man's heart
I can bear only pain.

Only you are the child
I can give strength enough
to fight this injustice.

Nine Months After
I Began Writing

March 1817

A slice of moon rises to light the black March sky.
Shelley, Claire and the children are sleeping
as I coax the last words from my feathered quill
and complete my story.

My belly quickens with the child I carry,
but I feel as if a long labour is over
and my eyes are peering into the eyes
of a new offspring,

those of my Creature.

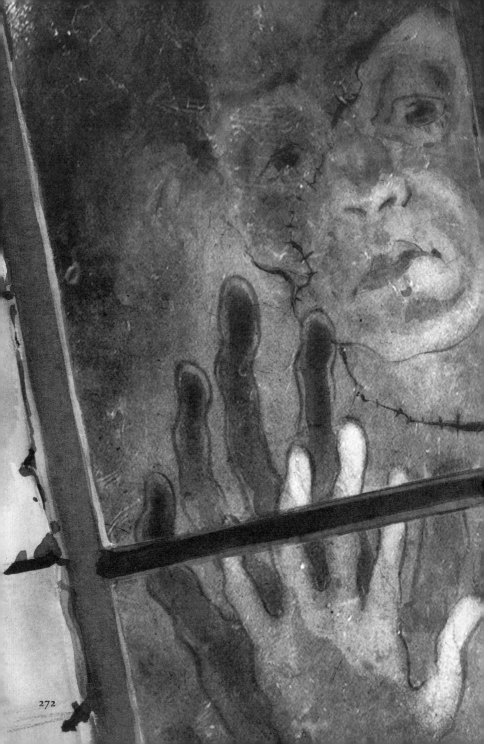

PART IX

An Ending

1818-1823

Forget the dead, the past? Oh, yet
There are ghosts that may take revenge for it;
Memories that make the heart a tomb,
Regrets which glide through the spirit's gloom,
And with ghastly whispers tell
That joy, once lost, is pain.

- Percy Bysshe Shelley, *The Past*, 1818

Anonymous

Anonymous,

I publish my book four months after my second
      daughter, Clara,
named after her dead sister, is born.

Anonymous,

because the publisher insists readers will never buy it
if they know a woman wrote it.

Anonymous,

just like my unnamed Creature.

FRANKENSTEIN;

OR,

THE MODERN PROMETHEUS.

IN THREE VOLUMES.

Did I request thee, Maker, from my clay
To mould me man?   Did I solicit thee
From darkness to promote me?——
PARADISE LOST.

VOL. I.

London:
PRINTED FOR
LACKINGTON, HUGHES, HARDING, MAVOR, & JONES,
FINSBURY SQUARE.

1818.

SUNKEN HOPE

MARCH 1818

Reviewers loathe *Frankenstein*
and condemn its author
for *his* atheistic beliefs.
I grow afraid of being discovered
and having their hatred directed toward me.
Though secretly,
I rejoice too in their heated discussions,
because my work isn't ignored.

Shelley isn't so fortunate.
Like his earlier works, critics ignore his new poem,
  The Revolt of Islam.
Instead of reviewing his writing, they target him
  with witch hunts
for his 'immoral behaviour' and openly accuse him
of having driven Harriet to suicide.

We are forced to flee,
this time to Italy,
when Londoners unleash hatred
viler than we've ever felt before.

Under a Burning Sun

Suddenly my life with Shelley
feels like terrible motion,
never finding home,
only running,
endlessly running.

It's as if happiness lies just over that cypress-studded ridge
or that sun-drenched sea.

We drift from one marble palazzo and overflowing gallery
of Renaissance paintings and lemon
orchard and shaded olive grove and medieval
church and crumbling Roman ruin to the next.

Shelley holds on to his belief that art
can lift the world out of despair,
but I am no longer moored by his faith that poetry and politics
are of greater importance than relationships between people.

I have no more dreams
to soar alongside his.

My soul is anchored
under the wide, bare sands of the Venetian Lido,
where we must bury our second daughter, Clara,
without erecting a tombstone,
because Shelley is in a hurry
to move on.

CURSED

I feel as if I am living alongside my Creature,
pursued and cursed
by the ghosts of Fanny and Harriet.

Cursed when I witnessed Claire's anguish
after we handed over her baby, Alba, to Byron.

Cursed when I felt Clara's body burn with fever
and grow limp in my arms
when death stole her from me.

Cursed to endure the agony that now I can do nothing
to prevent our son, William, from sickening with malaria
and following his sisters to the grave.

Cursed to live this unbearable existence
while those I love
die.

FOREBODING

MAY 1822

After wandering through Italy for four years,
we have come to live
in an isolated house on the Bay of Lerici,
where Shelley has asked his new friends,
Edward and Jane Williams, to join us.

We have another infant son
we have named Percy,
and Shelley and I both are writing again.
I pray happiness can find us here.

But Percy's beautiful life only makes me worry
there are more dreadful things yet to come.

The longer we stay in this damp little house,
the longer I hear the sea lashing,
lashing against the rocky beach,
the longer the waves seep under our door,
the more I feel
foreboding.

I Am Helpless

I fear we will not escape
the destiny I gave my unloved Creature.

Shelley's demons turn his thoughts murderous.
At night he wakes me from sleep,
screaming that he dreamed his hands were gripping my neck,
strangling me.

His poetry is filled with images of the dead.
He hallucinates nightmarish visions
of bloodied people standing atop the sea,
their eyes hollow,
their bones showing through their skin.

I can do nothing but watch
as he becomes completely disillusioned.
Life and love are only mirages to him.
It is death alone that holds his fascination.

I must turn toward living and keeping our son safe.
I no longer beg Shelley to stay when he sails
with Edward into another restless sea,
even though I know he dares the wind
to show him the mysteries that haunt him
about what lies beyond the grave.

Day after day
I wait.

But he does not return.

BETWEEN DREAMS AND ASHES

Edward's body is found first,
and then I know.

Ten days after they disappeared
I learn that Shelley's decayed and ruined corpse
has washed up on shore.
Only his clothes and a volume of poems he carries in his pocket
identify him.

Now Byron and the men who gathered for the search
prevent me from attending his funeral.
But they can't protect me
from reliving this ugly nightmare burning through my imagination.

This is the same nightmare
my Creature desires for himself
at the end of my novel.

Smoke, stench, a pyre of flame.
Shelley's once-beautiful body
is blackened ash swept out to sea.
I am twenty-four,
widowed,
alone.

No More Let Life Divide

I am given the blackened, charred remains
of his suffering heart
and wrap them within a page
from one of his poems, *Adonaïs*,
and with one last, lingering kiss, I whisper his line
  'No more let life divide what death can join together.'

Now Shelley has gone to a place where hatred
and pain can no longer reach him.
And I am free to love him eternally.

I place the poem within my writing desk,
alongside the journals we began together
when we ran across France in search of a world
that was yet to exist.

SISTERS NO MORE

1823

After everything we've been through,
after all the battles to love each other
alongside Shelley,
after anger and jealousy and betrayal,
I cannot share the part of Shelley
that remains to me now.

Claire believes he loved her more than me,
and I must grieve alone.
I part from her, pack my few belongings
and board a ship with my son, Percy,
to go home to England.

REDEMPTION

I have come home to find my Creature
is the centre of attention!

Frankenstein has been adapted into a play.
Audiences are pouring into theatres.
Playgoers recoil in horror as my Creature
bursts on stage with a crash of thunder.
Oh, how they love being frightened by him!

Angry placard bearers march London streets
trying to block this 'vile and monstrous drama.'
But their threats only excite people's curiosity
about my book.

I feel redeemed.
My creation stands on the threshold
of immortality.
We can affect the lives of generations to come,
if we are brave enough to open the wings of our imagination
and create!

A Hard, but Beautiful Existence

Byron has made public letters that prove
I wrote *Frankenstein*.
I am no longer anonymous!
I still choose a quiet life away from gossip,
but I have a small circle of friends.

I edit Shelley's unpublished poems.
At last, readers see his genius
and allow the light he held up to the world
to enter their hearts.

I survive. I keep writing.
I am scarred by my years with Shelley,
but he believed in me.
He inspired me to create.
And that gave me strength.

I have made terrible mistakes.
I must endure the knowledge that others
were swallowed by darkness because of my actions.
I have witnessed the wreckage of cruelty.
But unlike my father, I will never be consumed
by bitterness and anger.
I have released those monsters on to the page.

By creating, I keep faith alive
that we will learn someday
to cast aside cruelty and hatred
and build a just world
filled with love.

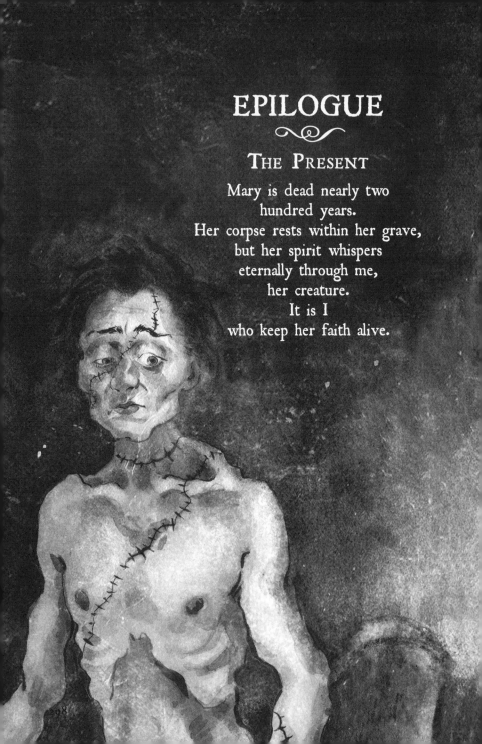

EPILOGUE

THE PRESENT

Mary is dead nearly two
hundred years.
Her corpse rests within her grave,
but her spirit whispers
eternally through me,
her creature.
It is I
who keep her faith alive.

More About Mary Shelley and
Frankenstein

By 1823, when Mary returned to England, five different adaptations of *Frankenstein* had appeared on-stage, and it was soon playing over much of the globe. Mary never made a penny from these productions because copyright laws weren't in place. In 1910, the first motion picture version appeared, and since then, *Frankenstein* has inspired countless creative works.

Mary created the first industrial-age science fiction novel as well as the first 'mad scientist', a character archetype that is utilised in many modern stories. The ideas in *Frankenstein* grew from lectures she attended; extensive reading; discussions with Shelley, Byron and Polidori; and her knowledge of grisly experiments being performed on executed convicts from Newgate Prison. In 1803, an anatomy professor named Giovanni Aldini attached metal plates to a deceased criminal's body and then applied electrical current, contorting the corpse's muscles. The dead man's fists clenched, his arm lifted and beat violently against the table, and one eye even opened. This and other galvanism experiments were graphically recorded in the press, causing such public outcry that the practice was banned in 1805. The brutal imagery was worked directly into Mary's own scene of Dr Frankenstein bringing a corpse back to life. Her vision of the use of galvanism was a plausible prediction of what scientists believed they would eventually accomplish - resurrecting the dead through the use of electricity. It's not that far off the mark when we consider how doctors use the electrical paddles of a defibrillator to shock a heart attack victim's heart back into a regular rhythm.

In an era of heated debate about humanity's relationship to nature and God, Mary's Creature was also conceived as a caution to men who assume too much power over nature. The warning still holds surprising relevance today, when ethical debates swirl around genetically modified crops, recombinant DNA technology, cloning, cloud seeding and genetic screening of human fetuses.

The severe electrical storms and distressing weather that the Shelleys experienced while staying at the Villa Diodati also fueled their discussions on galvanism. That year, 1816, was considered the year without a summer because the eruption in 1815 of Indonesia's Mount Tambora formed a dense ash cloud that circled the globe. It was one of the most violent eruptions in recorded history, and the crop failures and famines resulting from the volcanic winter were felt all over the world.

Mary Shelley's novel also challenged the idea that men alone, without women, could create life with their own hands, overruling the laws of nature. She depicted her creature as motherless, like herself. The story not only reflects Mary's own longing for her mother, but also echoes the searing heartache and anger she experienced when her father rejected her for living a life like the one he had promoted - Mary had been strongly influenced by Godwin's proud and open account of her mother's having had an illegitimate child with a married man. Mary was also deeply hurt by Shelley's lack of grief when their first daughter died. She had seen fathers reject their children, and suggested that evil will reign in a world where life is created by men alone.

With her writing and her life, Mary defied the restrictions put on women, and for two hundred years her Creature has lived on to inspire new stories, films, plays and artwork, as well as ethical debates about the role of science. *Frankenstein* is a testament to the teenage Mary Shelley's strength and enduring genius.

AUTHOR'S NOTE

The popular myth is that Mary Shelley's *Frankenstein* was conceived spontaneously on a stormy night in answer to a dare to write a ghost story. That evening did occur, but countless events in Mary's life before and after that evening played a much greater role in the horror novel's creation. My story is an attempt to trace the many origins of her genius. It's a testament to a resilient girl whose imagination, forged by isolation, persecution and loss, created a new form of storytelling as a means of connecting with the very society that had socially exiled her.

In my own life, I have faced obstacles that made the act of creating difficult. None were as challenging as Mary's, but a chronic autoimmune condition caused a long period of illness and denied me the use of my hands, feet and eyes. During this time, extreme pain and fatigue imposed feelings of loss and isolation. And yet, the urgent desire to create is what spurred me to fight back and regain my strength during difficult periods of physical therapy and chemotherapy. Throughout those years, my search to uncover Mary's story fueled my recovery. Her example gave me strength, and her story inspired me to search for a unique form of storytelling using both pictures and poems.

My book is structured in nine parts as tribute to the nine months Mary spent writing the complete draft of her novel. The significance of the length of the gestation period for her story - the same as that for an infant - was not lost on her; she frequently referred to her novel *Frankenstein* as her 'offspring' or 'progeny'. Also, part of the narrative of *Frankenstein* is told through a series of dated letters. The date of the first letter coincides with the date of Mary's own conception (as recorded in her father's diary), while the last letter is written nine months later, bearing the same date as Mary's mother's funeral a few days after her birth.

I have represented the details of Mary's life by weaving the actual events (as documented in her journals, copious letters and later biographies) with the themes she and Shelley wrote about in their creative work. Having grown up the daughter of two incredibly famous people, Mary was acutely aware that her life with Shelley would be historically scrutinised. She recorded her life in a series of journals, describing in great detail the books she and Shelley read, where they travelled, what they discussed and even when they made love. In some instances, I have omitted events in her life in order to focus on those that I think directly influenced the creation of *Frankenstein*. Her actual conversations with others have been lost to time, of course, but the dialogue within this story is constructed from the available letters and journals. Yet, despite the prodigious historical record, some details remain cloaked in mystery, most notably whether Shelley had a physical affair with Claire. I drew the conclusion that he did, because Shelley endorsed 'free love' and communal living and Claire fuelled rumours of their affair after his death. But the most convincing evidence was that pages of Mary's journal during the time when Shelley and Claire's bond was most intense were ripped out. Most historians have come to the same conclusions.

I did not include Mary and Shelley's marriage following Harriet's suicide because I don't believe the legalisation of their union was a momentous event to either of them. Shelley wanted to legalise their relationship solely to help his ill-fated attempt to gain custody of his children by Harriet. The wedding was by no means a romantic gesture made out of love. Shelley mocked the marriage in a letter to Claire as 'insignificant'. Mary recorded the date inaccurately in her diary by writing, 'A marriage takes place on the 29th,' when in fact they were married in a brief ceremony at St Mildred's Church on 30 December 1816.

It may be difficult to understand why Mary stayed in what any modern person would deem an extremely abusive relationship. But Mary grew up in a time when abusive relationships were far from abnormal. She had no role model for how a successful bond between a man and woman functioned. Furthermore, she had been raised to want a life beyond the bounds of convention. As a brilliant young girl, she had few options for undertaking a life that would be intellectually rewarding. Shelley offered her an extraordinary opportunity. He not only cherished her brilliance, but also esteemed her work as that of an equal in a time when hardly any man would have done the same. Though she suffered greatly by his infidelity and erratic behaviour, I believe she had empathy for him and his own inner turmoil. Even after his death, she remained resolute in her love for him and devoted the remainder of her life to championing his poetry, editing his writing, and tirelessly working to have it published. Her efforts made Shelley's writing endure.

It may also be difficult to read that Claire didn't fight to keep her daughter, but she could have done nothing to prevent Byron from claiming her. She had no income and she knew the courts recognised a father's right over that of a mother's. Allegra died of fever at the age of five, and Claire hated Byron for the rest of her life. Despite Claire's bitter feelings, Shelley resumed a deep friendship with Byron during the years he and Mary lived in Italy.

What Became of Them

George Gordon Noel, 6th Baron Byron (1788-1824), known as Lord Byron, is regarded as one of the great Romantic poets. His poems *Don Juan*, *Childe Harold's Pilgrimage* and *She Walks in Beauty* remain widely read. During his lifetime, his incredible fame was tarnished by scandals over personal excesses and huge debts, numerous love affairs, a heated divorce and rumours of a sexual liaison with his half sister. Shortly after Shelley's death, Byron went to Greece to join in the Greek War for Independence against the Ottoman Empire, but soon died of fever at the age of thirty-six.

Claire Clairmont (1798-1879) was born Clara Mary Jane Clairmont, the second child of Mary Jane Clairmont. Her mother identified her father as Charles Clairmont and adopted the name Clairmont herself to disguise Claire's illegitimacy. Claire was actually called Jane as a child, though for simplicity I referred to her as Claire for the entirety of the book. She changed her name shortly after running away with Mary and Shelley. Claire never married. After Shelley's death she worked in Russia as a governess, in Germany as a housekeeper and then in England as a music teacher. She moved back to Italy in 1841 and outlived her stepsister by twenty-eight years.

Mary Jane Clairmont Godwin (1766-1841) was the mother of Charles and Claire Clairmont and the second wife of William Godwin. Though deeply hostile toward her stepchildren, she was an intelligent businesswoman who worked closely with her husband in their business, M. J. Godwin & Co., to establish one of the first bookstores for children's literature. She was the only female publisher in London in the early 1800s.

William Godwin (1756-1836) was a journalist, philosopher and novelist. His most famous books were *An Enquiry Concerning Political Justice*, and his mystery novel *Things as They Are; or, The Adventures of Caleb Williams*. Held up as a symbol of radical thought throughout the 1790s, he was later abandoned by most of his supporters due to the rising tide of political conservatism. After he married his second wife, Mary Jane Clairmont, he wrote children's books on biblical and historical tales. His pioneering writing is often overshadowed by the scandal of his later years, when, burdened by insurmountable debts, he was forced to borrow heavily from Shelley and Mary.

Frances 'Fanny' Imlay (1794-1816), known as both Fanny Godwin and Frances Wollstonecraft, was the illegitimate daughter of American commercial speculator Gilbert Imlay and British feminist Mary Wollstonecraft. Fanny's father left her mother in France in the midst of the French Revolution, shortly after Fanny's birth. Fanny committed suicide at the age of twenty-two.

John William Polidori (1795-1821) trained as a doctor but yearned to be a writer. In 1816 he entered Lord Byron's service as his personal physician. Unbeknownst to Byron, Polidori was also being paid £500 by an English publisher to keep a diary detailing Byron's activities. Polidori and Byron's relationship was tempestuous, and the doctor was soon dismissed. His unhappy life spiralled out of control in 1819 when he published *The Vampyre*, a story he wrote while staying at the Villa Diodati. Without his consent, the publisher, seeking commercial success, credited Byron as the author. Polidori could do nothing about the injustice due to the copyright laws of the time. Byron was infuriated and publicly scorned Polidori's writing. Despite the fact that he had written the first modern vampire story, Polidori's literary career was ruined and his mental state became increasingly erratic. Weighed down by depression and gambling debts, he committed suicide by swallowing prussic acid (cyanide) at the age of twenty-five.

Mary Wollstonecraft Shelley's (1797-1851) novel *Frankenstein; or, The Modern Prometheus* (1818) has remained in print for two hundred years. She wrote other novels, short stories, essays and travel accounts. Her historical novels include *Valperga* (1823), *The Fortunes of Perkin Warbeck* (1830), *The Last Man* (1826), *Lodore* (1835) and *Falkner* (1837). She also worked tirelessly to edit and publish Percy Shelley's work, ensuring his place as one of the greatest poets of the English language.

In 1848, her son, Percy Florence, married Jane Gibson St John. Mary found happiness at last living with them, but her last ten years were fraught with illness. She died of a brain tumour at the age of fifty-three. On the first anniversary of her death, her son opened her desk and found within it locks of her dead children's hair, a notebook she had shared with Percy Bysshe Shelley, and a copy of his poem *Adonaïs*, with one page folded around a silk parcel. It contained the charred remains of Shelley's heart, pulled from the funeral pyre in Italy.

Percy Bysshe Shelley (1792-1822) has come to be regarded as one of the greatest poets of the Romantic era. Most publishers refused to publish his work during his lifetime for fear of being arrested for blasphemy or sedition. Recognition for his poetry grew steadily following his death due to Mary Shelley's untiring effort to have his work published. Eventually he became an idol among poets. His poem *The Mask of Anarchy* has been called the greatest poem of non-violent political protest ever written. Other major works include the long visionary poems: *Queen Mab*, *Alastor*, *The Revolt of Islam* and *Adonaïs*.

Mary Wollstonecraft (1759-1797) was a writer, philosopher and advocate of women's rights. During her brief career, she wrote novels, travel narratives, a history of the French Revolution and a children's book. She was celebrated for her essay *A Vindication of the Rights of Woman*. The publication of William Godwin's biography after her death, which illuminated her unorthodox life, had a devastating impact on her reputation. Her work was vilified by many for almost a century after. However, with the emergence of the feminist movement at the turn of the twentieth century, readers rediscovered her wisdom and turned to her advocacy of women's rights. Today she is considered a founder of the feminist movement.

WHAT WERE THEY READING?

This list is derived from *The Journals of Mary Shelley: 1814-1844*, Paula R. Feldman and Diana Scott-Kilvert, eds. (Oxford: Clarendon Press, 1987).

Author	Title	Published
Adolphus, John	*Biographical Memoirs of the French Revolution*	1799
Aeschylus	*Prometheus Vinctus*	
	Bible New Testament	
Byron, George Gordon, Lord	*The Corsair: A Tale*	1814
Byron, George Gordon, Lord	*Childe Harold's Pilgrimage*	1812
Coleridge, Samuel Taylor	*The Rime of the Ancient Mariner*	1798
Davy, Sir Humphrey	*Elements of Chemical Philosophy*	1812
Godwin, William	*Fleetwood; or, the New Man of Feeling*	1805
Godwin, William	*An Enquiry Concerning Political Justice*	1793
Goethe, Johann Wolfgang von	*The Sorrows of Werther*	1774
Milton, John	*Paradise Lost*	1667
Milton, John	*Paradise Regained*	1671
Rousseau, Jean-Jacques	*Les Confessions*	1782
Rousseau, Jean-Jacques	*Émile*	1762
Scott, Walter	*The Lady of the Lake*	1810
Shelley, Percy Bysshe	*Queen Mab*	1813
Staël-Holstein, Mme Germaine de	*De l'Allemagne*	1810
Voltaire	*Candide*	1759
Wollstonecraft, Mary	*A Vindication of the Rights of Woman*	1792
Wollstonecraft, Mary	*Maria or, The Wrongs of Woman*	1798
Wordsworth, William	*The Excursion*	1814
Wordsworth, William	*Poems*	1815

NOTES

PART I: EXILE

Do Not Return, on the deck of the *Osnaburgh*, Seymour, 71.

Memories, My stepmother hadn't even come, Godwin, *Diary*, Jun. 7, 1812.

Memories, easy prey to pickpockets and thieves, Seymour, 72.

Herschel's Comet, how he watched a comet, Seymour, 27.

Herschel's Comet, until she had named eight comets, Hoskin, 138-42.

A Childhood of Poems, independence is admirable, Seymour, 51-52.

Without a Word, he took her to church, Seymour, 45-46.

The New Mrs Godwin, She had been an unwed mother and … debtors' prison, Gordon, 28-29.

Debts, money enough to give to any friend in need, Seymour, 47.

No Longer My Home, crept beneath the couch … dragged me out by my hair, Seymour, 58.

Holborn, Mrs Godwin's idea … in Somers Town, Gordon, 32.

Father Wasn't Meant to Keep Shop, the first to call himself an anarchist, Seymour, 6-7.

Father Wasn't Meant to Keep Shop, a notorious radical, Gordon, 34.

Green-Eyed Devil, would do without singing lessons, Gordon, 50.

Green-Eyed Devil, green-tinted glasses, Mellor, 6.

Exile, she is the one who does all the screaming, Gordon, 50.

Penance, I am cursed by sea and sickness, Seymour, 71-72.

Because I Do, For ten days my mother battled to live, Godwin, *Diary*, 30 Aug - 10 Sept, 1797.

Six Days and Nights, wrote my father a letter … wanted to be of service to him, Cameron, 100-02.

PART II: MY SECOND BIRTH

A New Home, I am thankful … warmed by kindness, Mellor, 16.

Isabella, We walk to the high mound … harbour, Seymour, 74-76.

Isabella, 'O Liberty! What crimes are committed in thy name!' Gordon, 54.

Mother, braved mobs and bloody riots … revolution, Gordon, 183, 199-210.

Mother, the first to denounce unfair laws toward women, Gordon, 61-62.

The Books My Mother Wrote, Death may snatch me … path, Wollstonecraft, 101-02.

Almost Two Years, Father writes … strengthen my character, Godwin, *Diary*, 1812-1814, Seymour, 72.

PART III: RETURN TO DARKNESS

Return to Darkness, The allied armies … harmony to the whole world, Evans, 355.

An End to War, All of London is celebrating, Seymour, 87.

Chains, dared to hope that the French general … would bring reform, Seymour, 88.

A Spiritual Son, *He is the son of a wealthy baronet*, derived from Mellor, 17-19.

Part IV: The Poet

Part V: Six Weeks of Freedom

PART VII: WILD HEARTS

Part VIII: Deeper into Nightmares

Part IX: An Ending

BIBLIOGRAPHY

Cameron, Kenneth Neill, ed. *Shelley and His Circle, 1773-1822.* London: Oxford University Press, 1961.

Douglass, Paul. *Lady Caroline Lamb: A Biography.* New York: Palgrave Macmillan, 2004.

Evans, John. *A Sketch of the Denominations of the Christian World.* 18th ed. London: Longman, 1841.

Godwin, William. *The Diary of William Godwin.* Edited by Victoria Myers, David O'Shaughnessy, and Mark Philp. Oxford: Oxford Digital Library, 2010. godwindiary.bodleian.ox.ac.uk/index2.html.

——. *Memoirs of the Author of 'A Vindication of the Rights of Woman.'* London: J. Johnson and G. G. and Jo Robinson, 1798.

Gordon, Charlotte. *Romantic Outlaws: The Extraordinary Lives of Mary Wollstonecraft and Her Daughter Mary Shelley.* New York: Random House, 2015.

Holmes, Richard. *The Age of Wonder: How the Romantic Generation Discovered the Beauty and Terror of Science.* New York: Vintage Books, 2010.

——. *Shelley: The Pursuit.* New York: New York Review Books, 2003.

Hoskin, Michael A. *Discoverers of the Universe: William and Caroline Herschel.* Princeton, N.J.: Princeton University Press, 2011.

MacCarthy, Fiona. *Byron: Life and Legend.* New York: Farrar, Straus, and Giroux, 2002.

Mellor, Anne K. *Mary Shelley: Her Life, Her Fiction, Her Monsters.* New York: Routledge, 1989.

Scolfield, William [William Godwin]. *Bible Stories.* 2 vols. London: Richard Phillips, 1802.

Seymour, Miranda. *Mary Shelley.* New York: Grove Press, 2000.

Shelley, Mary Wollstonecraft. *The Annotated Frankenstein.* Edited by Susan J. Wolfson and Ronald Levao. Cambridge, Mass.: Belknap Press of Harvard University Press, 2012.

——. *Frankenstein: The Lynd Ward Illustrated Edition.* Edited by Lynd Ward. Mineola, NY: Dover, 2009.

——. *The Journals of Mary Shelley: 1814-1844.* Edited by Paula R. Feldman and Diana Scott-Kilvert. Oxford: Clarendon Press, 1987.

——. *The Letters of Mary Wollstonecraft Shelley.* Edited by Betty Bennett. Baltimore: Johns Hopkins University Press, 1980.

Shelley, M. W. 'Frankenstein, Volume I', in The Shelley-Godwin Archive, MS. Abinger c. 56, 21r. Retrieved from http://shelleygodwinarchive.org/sc/oxford/frankenstein/volume/i/#/p44/mode/img

Shelley, Percy Bysshe. *The Letters of Percy Bysshe Shelley.* Edited by Frederick Jones. Oxford: Clarendon Press, 1964.

——. *Shelley's Poetry and Prose: Authoritative Texts, Criticism.* New York: Norton, 2002.

Stott, Andrew McConnell. *The Poet and the Vampyre: The Curse of Byron and the Birth of Literature's Greatest Monsters.* New York: Pegasus Books, 2004.

Wollstonecraft, Mary. *Maria, or, The Wrongs of Woman: A Posthumous Fragment.* Philadelphia: James Carey, 1799.

Wroe, Ann. *Being Shelley: The Poet's Search for Himself.* London, Vintage, 2008.

ACKNOWLEDGMENTS

My deepest thanks are to my husband, Dave, who had faith that I could complete this project even before I had it in myself. You always know when to push me to be better than I think I can be.

And my agent, Linda Pratt, whose boundless generosity and enthusiasm for this project kept my passion fuelled during four long years of working on this book. Truly, I couldn't have done this without you.

And for Connie Hsu, my brilliant and patient editor. Thank you for seeing the potential in this book and for helping me weave a thousand thoughts into the story I had hoped to create.

Thank you, too, Simon Boughton, Roberta Pressel, Megan Abbate, Karen Ninnis, Nancy Elgin, Angela Corbo Gier and the whole amazing team at Roaring Brook, who invested their creativity and energy in this project. I am blessed to have my books in your hands.

And my deepest gratitude to Karen and Randy Hesse for offering countless helpful comments on early drafts and for being a safe harbour where I could land during the years of work. Karen, I write because your passion ignited my own.

Thank you also to my early readers, Julie Reimer, Meg Kearney and Kristin Cashore, for your very helpful comments. And to my writing group - Jackie Davies, Ali Benjamin, Leslie Connor, Grace Lin, and Molly Burnham - whose moral support and wisdom helped me get through to the end. I am grateful to Dr Bruce Barker-Benfield, curator of the Shelley collections at the Bodleian Library in Oxford, for giving me access to Mary's original journals and manuscripts.

Lastly, a huge thanks to Ingrid Aho and Eva Goldfinger for doing a wonderful job posing as models for the illustrations of Mary, Claire and Fanny.